Lasting Legacy:

making a difference with my life

Bible Study That Builds Christian Community

SERENDIPITY
H O U S E

LIFE
CONNECTIONS

To order additional copies of this resource:
ORDER ONLINE at *www.serendipityhouse.com*;
VISIT the LifeWay Christian Store serving you;
WRITE Serendipity House
117 10th Avenue, North
Nashville, TN 37234
FAX (615) 277-8181
PHONE (800) 525-9563

Printed in the United States of America

117 10th Avenue, North
Nashville, Tennessee 37234

Contents

Core Values

Community: The purpose of this curriculum is to build community within the body of believers around Jesus Christ.

Group Process: To build community, the curriculum must be designed to take a group through a step-by-step process of sharing your story with one another.

Interactive Bible Study: To share your "story," the approach to Scripture in the curriculum needs to be open-ended and right-brained—to "level the playing field" and encourage everyone to share.

Developmental Stages: To provide a healthy program in the life cycle of a group, the curriculum needs to offer courses on three levels of commitment:

    (1) **Beginner Level**—low-level entry, high structure, to level the playing field;

    (2) **Growth Level**—deeper Bible study, flexible structure, to encourage group accountability;

    (3) **Discipleship Level**—in-depth Bible study, open structure, to move the group into high gear.

Target Audiences: To build community throughout the culture of the church, the curriculum needs to be flexible, adaptable, and transferable into the structure of the average church.

Mission: To expand the kingdom of God one person at a time by filling the "empty chair." (We add an extra chair to each group session to remind us of our mission.)

4

Group Covenant

It is important that your group covenant together, agreeing to live out important group values. Once these values are agreed upon, your group will be on its way to experiencing Christian community. It's very important that your group discuss these values—preferably as you begin this study. The first session would be most appropriate. (Check the rules to which each member of your group agrees.)

☐ **Priority:** While you are in this course of study, you give the group meetings priority.

☐ **Participation:** Everyone is encouraged to participate and no one dominates.

☐ **Respect:** Everyone is given the right to his or her own opinion, and all questions are encouraged and respected.

☐ **Confidentiality:** Anything that is said in the meeting is never repeated outside the meeting.

☐ **Life Change:** We will regularly assess our own life-change goals and encourage one another in our pursuit of Christlikeness.

☐ **Empty Chair:** The group stays open to reaching new people at every meeting.

☐ **Care and Support:** Permission is given to call upon each other at any time, especially in times of crisis. The group will provide care for every member.

☐ **Accountability:** We agree to let the members of the group hold us accountable to the commitments we make in whatever loving ways we decide upon.

☐ **Mission:** We will do everything in our power to start a new group.

☐ **Ministry:** The group will encourage one another to volunteer and serve in a ministry and to support missions by giving financially and/or personally serving.

For the Leader

Each group meeting consists of a three-part agenda:

Icebreaker – Fun questions designed to warm the group and build understanding about other group members. These questions prepare the group for meaningful discussion throughout the session.

Bible Study – The heart of each session is the Bible study time. The Life Connections series involves six easy-to-understand segments.

1. **Scripture Reading** – Each Bible study begins with the reading of the focal passage.
2. **About Today's Session** – This section of the Bible Study time is designed to peak the interest of attendees and introduce the theme for the session. In most instances there will be a reminder of what was studied the previous week, a captivating illustration or analogy related to everyday life, and a statement describing what life-changing topic will be given attention.
3. **Identifying with the Story** – During this segment of the Bible Study, subgroups learn more about each other by answering questions that will help them share their story. These questions directly relate to the topic for the day.
4. **Today's Session** – This short teaching time will be led by the Master Teacher. These scripted teachings include a depth of biblical understanding, fascinating illustrations, analogies, statistics, and stories that will spark questions and conviction.
5. **Learning from the Story** – Subgroups will gather to answer a series of questions that anticipate commitment to applying the truths taught.
6. **Life Change Lessons** – The Master Teacher gives practical suggestions that will aid attendees in carrying out the commitments they make.

Caring Time – All study should point us to action. Each session ends with prayer and direction in caring for the needs of group members. Time is also provided to pray for the "empty chair." The empty chair is a visible symbol of the need for each group to lead an unbeliever to a relationship with Jesus Christ.

The cross icon and boxed text represents portions of the student book that have been reprinted in this book.

Every Life Connections group must fill three important roles. Each responsibility is vital to the success of the class.

Teacher – The teacher is the key leader of any Life Connections group. It is the responsibility of the teacher to:

1. enlist facilitators and apprentices.
2. make facilitators and apprentices aware of their roles and be certain these responsibilities are carried out.
3. meet periodically with facilitators to train, encourage, and inspire them.
4. cast vision for and keep the group focused on the goals of the group.
5. guide group members to understand and commit to the group covenant.
6. be sure the group utilizes, fills, and evangelizes through use of the empty chair concept.
7. act as the Master Teacher for the group.
8. keep the group on task throughout each session.

Facilitator – Each subgroup will have a facilitator. It is the responsibility of the facilitators to:

1. lead each individual in their subgroup to participate in Icebreaker activities.
2. involve all members in their subgroup in the Identifying with the Story section of the study.
3. guide those in their subgroup to commit to apply the lessons learned in the Learning from the Story section of the weekly session.
4. with sensitivity and wisdom lead their subgroup to minister to one another during the Caring Time and involve their subgroup in ministry and evangelism.
5. minister to the needs of their subgroup members and lead them to minister to the needs of one another both during and between meetings.

Apprentice – Every subgroup must have an apprentice. When the group consistently has eight or more in attendance, the group should divide into two groups. The apprentice will become the facilitator of the new group and choose an apprentice who will someday be the facilitator of a group. It is the role of the apprentice to:

1. learn from the facilitator of their group.
2. make welcome all new subgroup members.
3. be certain student books and pens or pencils are available for all participants.
4. turn in prayer requests.
5. encourage participation by actively participating themselves.
6. lead the group when the facilitator is unavailable.

For more information and frequently asked questions about Life Connections, visit our Web site at *www.serendipityhouse.com*.

Session

1

Sharing My Spiritual Story

Prepare for the Session

	READINGS	REFLECTIVE QUESTIONS
Monday	Galatians 1:11–12	Reflect on the time when you first heard the good news about Jesus and what He could do for you.
Tuesday	Galatians 1:13–14	What was your life like before knowing Christ?
Wednesday	Galatians 1:15–17	How did your life change after you chose to become a Christian?
Thursday	Galatians 1:18–20	Who helped you learn more and directed you to become more like Christ when you were a new believer?
Friday	Galatians 1:21–22	Who do you know who needs Jesus?
Saturday	Galatians 1:23	What do people say about your values, your character, and your actions?
Sunday	Galatians 1:24	Take time to praise God for the grace you have received.

notes:

OUR GOALS FOR THIS SESSION ARE:

In groups of 6–8, gather people in a horseshoe configuration.

Make sure everyone has a name tag.

Take time to share information on class parties that are coming up as well as any relevant church events.

INTRODUCE THE ICEBREAKER ACTIVITY: The students have been given instructions in their books.

After the Icebreaker say something like, "Sharing facts about our past starts the process of our getting to know each other. But even more important are our feelings about our past, especially in relation to the spiritual changes we have been through. That is what we will be looking at today."

Hand out the Prayer/Praise Report. A sample copy is on pages 158-159. Have people write down prayer requests and praises. Then have the prayer coordinator collect the report and make copies for use during the Caring Time.

BIBLE STUDY
- to learn how Paul told other people his story of how he became a Christian
- to understand the importance of sharing our own spiritual stories
- to look at some elements to include when we share our spiritual stories

LIFE CHANGE
- to listen to the spiritual stories of two mature Christians this week
- to write out in 250 words or less our spiritual stories
- to learn to share our spiritual stories naturally and from memory by telling them to at least one other person this week

Icebreaker (10-15 minutes)

Where I'm Coming From. Mark an "X" on the following continuums to let us know "where you're coming from":

I was raised mostly in:

a small town · a big city

The atmosphere of my childhood home was for the most part:

tense and hostile · peaceful and loving

In terms of what our family had, I was:

deprived · privileged

My religious training was:

nonexistent · stifling

I learned to see the world mostly as:

dangerous · safe

notes:

LEARNING FROM THE BIBLE

GALATIANS 1:11–24

Have one or two class members, selected ahead of time, read the passage from Galatians.

Bible Study   (30-45 minutes)

The Scripture for this week:

¹¹*I want you to know, brothers, that the gospel I preached is not something that man made up.* ¹²*I did not receive it from any man, nor was I taught it; rather, I received it by revelation from Jesus Christ.*

¹³*For you have heard of my previous way of life in Judaism, how intensely I persecuted the church of God and tried to destroy it.* ¹⁴*I was advancing in Judaism beyond many Jews of my own age and was extremely zealous for the traditions of my fathers.* ¹⁵*But when God, who set me apart from birth and called me by his grace, was pleased* ¹⁶*to reveal his Son in me so that I might preach him among the Gentiles, I did not consult any man,* ¹⁷*nor did I go up to Jerusalem to see those who were apostles before I was, but I went immediately into Arabia and later returned to Damascus.*

¹⁸*Then after three years, I went up to Jerusalem to get acquainted with Peter and stayed with him fifteen days.* ¹⁹*I saw none of the other apostles—only James, the Lord's brother.* ²⁰*I assure you before God that what I am writing you is no lie.* ²¹*Later I went to Syria and Cilicia.* ²²*I was personally unknown to the churches of Judea that are in Christ.* ²³*They only heard the report: "The man who formerly persecuted us is now preaching the faith he once tried to destroy."* ²⁴*And they praised God because of me.*

Summarize these introductory remarks. Be sure to include the underlined information, which gives the answers to the student book questions (provided in the margin).

According to this presentation, what is a gift only you can give?

What kind of feedback do we need to get from others?

...about today's session (5 minutes)

THE GIFT OF OUR STORIES

<u>One of the most unique and precious things we can share with another human being is the story of our spiritual journey. It's a gift nobody else can give.</u> Frederick Buechner writes in his book, *The Sacred Journey*, "The music of your life is subtle and elusive and like no other—not a song with words but a song without words, a singing, clattering music to gladden the heart or turn the heart to stone, to haunt you perhaps with echoes of a vaster, farther music of which it is a part."[1] The gift of our spiritual story is an important gift, because none of us can find our way in this life on our own. We need God's guidance, but we also need feedback from each other. <u>We need feedback on where other people have been, what wrong turns they have taken on their way, and how they arrived where they are now.</u> It's like an episode of the old TV show, *M*A*S*H**. Hawkeye amputated the leg of a man who stepped on a mine. Hawkeye

When has the story of someone else's journey helped you in your life?

asked later what happened. The man said he had figured he was approaching a mine field. Since it had snowed heavily, he followed in the tracks of someone who had gone before him. This had kept him safe until the footprints ended in mush. The man who had gone before him had hit a land mine, and now he was on his own. Even though knowing someone else's journey doesn't eliminate the dangers, it does help to know where someone else has been. That is the gift we can give each other.

1

⟳ Remain in groups of 6–8 people, in a horseshoe configuration.

In this small-group session, students will be responding to the following questions that will help them share their stories in terms of Paul's description of his conversion to Christ in Galatians 1:11–24.

Have the students explore these questions together.

✝ Identifying with the Story (5-7 minutes)

1. If you could point to one area of activity where, as a teenager, you were advancing beyond many of your own age, what area would it be?

   ☐ sports ☐ academics
   ☐ music ☐ knowledge of the Bible
   ☐ street smarts ☐ business acumen
   ☐ maturity ☐ dramatic ability
   ☐ verbal ability ☐ sophistication
   ☐ social confidence ☐ other:_____
   ☐ mechanical ability
   ☐ knowledge of my hobby area
   ☐ ability to get myself out of trouble

2. What do you remember doing as a youth that you are now ashamed of?

   ☐ lying to my parents
   ☐ teasing a kid in the neighborhood or at school
   ☐ being a racist
   ☐ teasing or hurting a sibling
   ☐ partying too much
   ☐ making fun of the Christian kids
   ☐ shoplifting
   ☐ other:_____

3. How would you describe your attitude toward God when you were a teen?

notes:

Share with your class the following information which you may modify according to your own perspectives and teaching needs. The answers to the student book questions (provided in the margin) are underlined.

today's session (15-20 minutes)

One of the earliest lessons we are taught in life is that "nice" kids share. Remember that? Many parents teach their kids that if they're going outside with a friend to play, and if they're planning to take a treat, like a cookie or ice cream bar, they should also take one to share with their friend. One of the hardest lessons brothers and sisters have to learn is how to share their toys. Some kids never learn that. Shel Silverstein wrote a poem about that, which is a take-off on an old bedtime prayer.

> *Now I lay me down to sleep,*
> *I pray the Lord my soul to keep,*
> *And if I die before I wake,*
> *I pray the Lord my toys to break.*
> *So none of the other kids can use 'em ... Amen.*[2]

The Importance of Sharing Ourselves

One of the most important things we can share is not our possessions, but ourselves—our stories that tell who we are. Like the child described in the poem, some of us have never learned to share ourselves. We would rather lose everything than open up to others.

Fortunately, Paul was not one who found it difficult to share his story with others. Most of us would have understood if he had such difficulty. After all, he participated in acts of violence that led to the imprisonment and death of innocent people. Some of those acts were passive, such as when he watched over the coats of those who stoned Stephen, the first Christian martyr (Acts 7:54–60). Some of his acts, however, were more active, such as when he headed to Damascus to arrest disciples (Acts 9:1–2). When he later became an

What things happened in Paul's life that could have made him hesitant to share his spiritual story with others?

evangelist for Christ, he had to work alongside many who probably had friends and relatives hurt by him. For example, Ananias hesitated to help Paul because he had heard about how much evil he had done (Acts 9:13–14). Faced with that kind of reaction, wouldn't it be natural for him to hesitate to tell his story to others? Also, most of us don't enjoy reliving our mistakes. We want to put them behind us and go on. But Paul *did* share his story, failures and all. He shared it for a couple of reasons. He shared it at this point because he wanted people to know his special authority for teaching the gospel. He also shared it because he knew God could use his story. God could use it to help others learn from his mistakes. Paul came to understand that what was most important was not what made him comfortable or made others see him in a good light, but what helped others see God as glorious and honorable (v. 24).

1

What to Share in Our Spiritual Stories

In telling his story, Paul gives us an example and shows us some elements that are helpful to include in sharing our own stories. Let's look at three such elements:

1. ***Tell how it used to be.*** Paul started by sharing how his life used to be before Christ came to him. He violently persecuted Christ and the church which he later came to love. This answers the essential question: "What was wrong that needed fixing?" Christians whose testimonies include turning from alcohol or drug addiction, crime, or any dramatic sins must learn to share such experiences so others going through such things can identify with them. However, some Christians have difficulty with this when it comes to telling the story of *their* spiritual journey. They have heard the testimonies of those Christ saved out of alcoholism, crime, or sexual promiscuity, and it just doesn't apply to them. They say, "I've always been a good kid and was raised in a Christian home. There was no big, dramatic turnaround." That is a common Christian story. But even then we have had some glimpses of what life is without Christ: We rebelled for a while or we let our passions pull us, at least enough toward "the dark side" that we saw what it was like before turning away. It is in such experiences that we learn for ourselves what is wrong and what needs to be fixed in the human condition. That is part of what we need to share with others.

We also need to share our gratitude for the good parts of our past. We can be thankful for our upbringing, realizing that we did nothing to earn such good fortune. Faithful parents are one of God's greatest gifts of grace.

What two reasons did Paul have for sharing his story with the Galatians?

What three elements does the leader encourage you to include when you tell your spiritual story?

What are some things people can share if they have been in the church all of their lives and were not saved out of a life of rebellion?

today's session (cont'd)

2. ***Tell what God did for you.*** Paul does this when he writes, "When God, who set me apart from birth and called me by his grace, was pleased to reveal his Son in me" (vv. 15–16). Here Paul recognizes the actions that brought about positive change in his life were God's. We should never make it appear that our status with God, or any positive change that has occurred in our lives, is something that we accomplished by our own merit, therefore making us a step above others who "haven't made it." Paul knew that the change in his life occurred solely by God's free gift of forgiveness. When we point out that our change came through God's grace, we help others realize that God can work the same changes in them as well, and that their own inadequacies will not thwart Him.

Why should you, when you tell your spiritual story, avoid making it look like positive changes in your life were the result of your own merit?

3. ***Tell what God has done through you to benefit others.*** Paul pointed out that because of what God did to change him, the Gentiles were able to receive the gospel, the good news of the death, burial, and resurrection of Jesus. Similarly, when God really changes us, He then uses us to benefit His church or others whom He loves. How has God's work in your life benefited others? Has it made you a better father, mother, or spouse? Has it given you a love for other Christians that you have sought to express in action? Has it helped you understand what it is like for strugglers? Our stories touch the stories of others—connecting all of us! An old hymn implores, "Make me a blessing to someone today!" That should be part of the story of each Christian.

notes:

Remain in groups of 6–8 people, in a horseshoe configuration.

In this small-group session, students will be applying the lessons of the text to their own lives through the following questions.

The students were asked (in the student book) to choose an answer for each question and explain why.

Learning from the Story (5-7 minutes)

1. What impression do you get of Paul from reading this story?

   ☐ He's an egotist.
   ☐ He "tells it like it is."
   ☐ He's not afraid of admitting his mistakes.
   ☐ He's too defensive.
   ☐ other:_____

2. When and how did God "reveal his Son" to you?

3. What has God done in your life recently for which others might glorify Him?

1

notes:

Share with the class the following thoughts on how the lessons of this text might be applied today. The answers to the student book questions (provided in the margin) are underlined unless the question requires a personal answer.

Why does sharing your spiritual story require some advance preparation?

What kind of words should you avoid in sharing your spiritual story?

life change lessons (5-7 minutes)

We need to go beyond talking about how Paul shared his story to sharing our own. Doing so effectively requires some thought in advance of when the opportunity comes. Otherwise we can end up stumbling through or sharing in a way that is not helpful. We have already looked at some of the elements we might include. Our preparation should also include the following:

1. LISTEN TO THE SPIRITUAL STORIES OF TWO MATURE CHRISTIANS THIS WEEK. Note how they share and which parts of their testimonies are most effective for you. With each faith story you listen to, note what kind of person would be most influenced by it.

2. WRITE OUT IN 250 WORDS OR LESS YOUR SPIRITUAL STORY. Include the elements we looked at in "Today's Session." Avoid words that would only be familiar to people who have been in the church for awhile. Picture the type of person who would be most influenced by your story and target what you write to him or her.

life change lessons (cont'd)

3. LEARN TO SHARE YOUR STORY NATURALLY AND FROM MEMORY BY TELLING IT TO ONE OTHER PERSON THIS WEEK. Don't make it sound like a speech from a telemarketer! Don't think you have to say things exactly the same every time. Say it naturally, and pause to let the other person respond to what you are saying. There's nothing worse than feeling like the other person is making a "canned" speech that you can't interrupt!

Caring Time (15-20 minutes)

This is the time for developing and expressing your caring for each other. Thank God for the changes He has brought about in people's lives. Begin to pray for others who need Christ in their lives. Pray that we will have the courage to share our stories. Pray for these concerns and any others that are listed in the Prayer/Praise Report.

notes:

⛑ CARING TIME
Remain in groups of 6–8 people, in a horseshoe configuration.

Hand out the Prayer/ Praise Report to the entire group. Ask each subgroup to pray for the empty chair. Pray specifically for God to guide you to someone to bring next week to fill that chair.

After a sufficient time of prayer in subgroups, close in a corporate prayer. Say, "Next week we will talk about: 'Being Vulnerable.' "

Remind participants of the daily Scripture readings and reflective questions found on page 18.

BIBLE STUDY NOTES

GALATIANS 1:11
family of faith

Reference Notes

Use these notes to gain further understanding of the text as you study on your own.

brothers. Paul's word for fellow Christians. Even though he later has harsh words for the Galatians, they are still part of the same family of faith. His words come with the awareness of his relationship and are laced with love for them personally.

GALATIANS 1:12
*head knowledge
becomes heart
knowledge*

GALATIANS 1:13
inner change

GALATIANS 1:14
Jewish law

GALATIANS 1:16
new purpose

GALATIANS 1:17
an apostle

GALATIANS 1:18
testimony

GALATIANS 1:19

GALATIANS 1:24

revelation. Literally, "an opening up of what was previously hidden." Paul had certainly heard the "facts" of the gospel prior to his conversion, but he had violently rejected them as blasphemous. It was only after Jesus Christ revealed the truth and meaning of these facts to him on the Damascus Road that he accepted the gospel.

my previous way of life. For other references to his previous way of life, see Acts 9:1–9 and 1 Timothy 1:13–16.

traditions of my fathers. In particular, this refers to the oral law developed to explain and apply the teaching of the Old Testament.

among the Gentiles. With Paul's conversion came his commission to preach to the Gentiles (Acts 9:15). In encountering Christ, he came to the realization that the Law was bankrupt (insofar as its ability to save anyone). Thus, there was no barrier preventing Gentiles from coming to Christ.

Apparently the Judaizers (Christians who were arguing that Gentile converts had to obey the Jewish ceremonial law) had been saying that after his conversion Paul had gone to Jerusalem and there received instructions about the gospel. That would have meant he received it secondhand, and therefore his teaching had less authority than that of the other apostles.
apostles before I was. The only distinction Paul admits between his apostleship and that of the leaders in Jerusalem is that of time. They were commissioned by Jesus earlier than he.
Arabia. In the tradition of Old Testament prophets and of Jesus after his baptism, Paul retreats to the desert for solitude and reflection.

Jerusalem. It was a courageous act by Paul to return here—to his former friends who might well try to harm him because of his conversion to Christianity, and to Christians who might not even receive him because of their suspicions about him.

to get acquainted. It was important that Paul come to know the leaders of the church. They, in turn, needed to hear a first-hand account of his conversion.

James. James eventually became the leader of the Jerusalem church. He was a strict and orthodox Jew (see Mark 6:3; Acts 1:14).

Even though the Judaizers in Galatia might be critical of Paul, the Christians in Judea praised God because of him.

notes:

[1] Fredrick Buechner, *The Sacred Journey* (San Francisco: Harper & Row, 1982), 77.
[2] Shel Silverstein, "Prayer of the Selfish Child" *A Light in the Attic* (New York: Harper & Row, 1981), 15.

Session

2

Being Vulnerable

Prepare for the Session

	READINGS	REFLECTIVE QUESTIONS
Monday	2 Corinthians 12:6	Why do we judge people by what they "do or say"?
Tuesday	2 Corinthians 12:6	How often do your words match your actions?
Wednesday	2 Corinthians 12:7–8	What would keep you from being conceited?
Thursday	2 Corinthians 12:7–8	Think about why you struggle with pride as a human being.
Friday	2 Corinthians 12:9	When has God's grace been sufficient for you?
Saturday	2 Corinthians 12:9	How do you know when the power of God is resting on you?
Sunday	2 Corinthians 12:10	Have you ever sensed the truth of this verse in your life?

notes:

OUR GOALS FOR THIS SESSION ARE:

In groups of 6–8, gather people in a horseshoe configuration.

Make sure everyone has a name tag.

Take time to share information on class parties that are coming up as well as any relevant church events.

BIBLE STUDY
- to consider Paul's view of what it means to have weaknesses
- to learn to be honest about our weaknesses
- to understand that in sharing our weaknesses, we can help others deal with their weaknesses

LIFE CHANGE
- to learn what others see as our weaknesses
- to schedule a quiet time where we submit our weaknesses to God and pray that He will show His strength through them
- to share our weaknesses with a close friend or in a small group of believers this week

Icebreaker (10-15 minutes)

Secret Identities. Depending on the amount of time you have, you may want to choose two of the following three questions to discuss:

1. Introduce yourself to others in your group by filling in the blanks in this statement: "Disguised as a mild-mannered *(your occupation)*, my secret identity, known previously to no other mortal is *(your favorite childhood superhero)*."

2. If you could retain only one super power, which one would you keep (and why)?

   ☐ faster than a speeding bullet
   ☐ able to leap tall buildings
   ☐ more powerful than a locomotive
   ☐ become invisible
   ☐ super ESP
   ☐ fly over my enemies
   ☐ x-ray vision
   ☐ can shrink or grow at will
   ☐ immortal
   ☐ other: _____

3. If you had the super power of being in two places at once, where else would you like to be right now?

INTRODUCE THE ICEBREAKER ACTIVITY:

The students have been given instructions in their books.

After the Icebreaker say something like, "While we may want to be invulnerable super beings, in reality we have many weaknesses. To share with other vulnerable human beings and have an influence on them, we have to be vulnerable ourselves. In this session we will be looking at what this means for us."

Hand out the Prayer/Praise Report. A sample copy is on pages 158-159. Have people write down prayer requests and praises. Then have the prayer coordinator collect the report and make copies for use during the Caring Time.

LEARNING FROM THE BIBLE

2 CORINTHIANS 12:6–10

Have a member of the class, selected ahead of time, read the passage from 2 Corinthians.

Bible Study (30-45 minutes)

The Scripture for this week:

⁶Even if I should choose to boast, I would not be a fool, because I would be speaking the truth. But I refrain, so no one will think more of me than is warranted by what I do or say.

⁷To keep me from becoming conceited because of these surpassingly great revelations, there was given me a thorn in my flesh, a messenger of Satan, to torment me. ⁸Three times I pleaded with the Lord to take it away from me. ⁹But he said to me, "My grace is sufficient for you, for my power is made perfect in weakness." Therefore I will boast all the more gladly about my weaknesses, so that Christ's power may rest on me. ¹⁰That is why, for Christ's sake, I delight in weaknesses, in insults, in hardships, in persecutions, in difficulties. For when I am weak, then I am strong.

notes:

Summarize these introductory remarks. Be sure to include the underlined information, which gives the answers to the student book questions (provided in the margin).

...about today's session (5 minutes)

BECOMING VULNERABLE

In the *Superman* movies of the 1980s, "the man of steel" was once again made popular by actor Christopher Reeve. Even though Superman had one area of vulnerability, Kryptonite, no one could defeat him. Some might come close enough to add some drama to the story, but he always prevailed. Many young men doubtlessly wished they could be like him. However, in one of the movies Superman determines that he wants to marry Lois Lane. It is then that he discovers a disturbing secret—in order to marry a human woman, he would have to give up his power and become vulnerable like everyone else. He does so and for the first time learns about pain when a big bruiser hits him in the jaw. The movie's symbolic message is clear—while it might be nice to be invulnerable, if we really want to relate to other human beings we have to be vulnerable ourselves. It is also significant that the one who played the man of steel was later injured in a horseback riding incident and became a quadriplegic. The strength and courage Christopher Reeve has shown as a vulnerable quadriplegic who has not given up on life far outshines any acts he did in fiction.

What mask does the leader urge you to remove?

What two reactions might people have if they don't see your need and vulnerability?

If we really want to show other people the power of God and the strength that can come through faith in Him, we must <u>remove any masks of our own invulnerability and strength</u>, and let people see that all we are and all we do comes from God. If people do *not* see our need and vulnerability, <u>they will not identify with us</u>, for they know *they* are weak and vulnerable. Conversely, if all they see is our natural strength, <u>they will not credit God</u> for what God has done in us. The apostle Paul knew that and that is why he showed his own vulnerability. In this session we will see how Paul did that and what it means for us.

2

notes:

☩

Identifying with the Story (5–7 minutes)

⊍ **Remain in groups of 6–8 people, in a horseshoe configuration.**

In this small-group session, students will be responding to the following questions that will help them share their stories in terms of Paul's words about his own weaknesses in 2 Corinthians 12:6–10.

Have the students explore these questions together.

1. Describe the attitude toward "boasting" in your home when you were a child by placing a mark on the following scale:

   ⋯⋯⋯⋯⋯⋯⋯⋯⋯⋯⋯⋯⋯⋯⋯⋯⋯⋯⋯⋯⋯
   1 2 3 4 5 6 7 8 9 10
   "Never toot your own horn!"   "If you've got it, flaunt it!"

2. Which of the following attitudes toward weakness or supposed weakness prevailed in your home when you were a child?

   ◯ big boys or girls don't cry
   ◯ admitting a weakness gives your enemies a chance to exploit it
   ◯ admitting a weakness is the first step in overcoming it
   ◯ sharing your feelings shows weakness
   ◯ other: _____

3. How do you feel about what Paul says here about weakness?

   ◯ confused—strength through weakness?
   ◯ irritated—He's just making excuses for himself!
   ◯ relieved—This means I can accept my weaknesses.
   ◯ other: _____

today's session (15-20 minutes)

In this life we have enemies. And when we realize we have enemies, our natural response is to shore up our defenses and hide the
weak areas the enemy might attack. In the Scripture story we are
looking at this week, Paul does not do that.

Paul's Enemies

Share with your
class the following
information which
you may modify
according to your
own perspectives
and teaching needs.
The answers to the
student book
questions (provided
in the margin) are
underlined.

Paul was writing to people who had been influenced by his
enemies and some who had become enemies themselves. They had
denigrated the authority he had as one of the apostles (1 Cor. 9:1–6).
They saw him as a fool (1 Cor. 4:9–10). They became secretive and
emotionally distant from him (2 Cor. 6:11–13). They criticized him
for being "bold" when he was away from them but "timid" when he
was with them face-to-face (2 Cor. 10:1). They even criticized his
appearance and speaking ability (2 Cor. 10:10).

*What were some of
the things that Paul's
enemies in Corinth
criticized about him?*

The natural reaction would have been for Paul not to give these
enemies any more ammunition! But that was not Paul's way. He
"opened wide" his heart to them (2 Cor. 6:11) and spoke frankly of
his weaknesses. He admitted that he was not a trained speaker (2
Cor. 11:6), and he spoke openly of a "thorn in my flesh" that had
caused him great grief (2 Cor. 12:7–9). If we take his other letters as
an example, he admitted to grave spiritual errors in his past (Gal.
1:13–14), and he spoke of his own struggles in doing what is right
(Rom. 7:7–25). Paul was not afraid to admit these weaknesses
because he believed that God was using them to His glory. Let's look at
some of the specific things Paul says about what his weaknesses meant.

Power in Weakness

*What message
did God give to
Paul about his
weaknesses?*

Paul reports that God gave him the message that " 'My grace is
sufficient for you, for my power is made perfect in weakness' " (v. 9).
Paul's whole message was to get people to depend more on God's
grace, his unmerited love and favor; and less on their own strength
and moral ability. He is saying, "God's grace is sufficient—there is no
need for you to be a physically perfect Superman; there is no need
to reinforce God's grace with the tactics people use when they don't
rely on that grace—tactics like boasting of their own abilities, denial
of their weaknesses, or showing defensiveness." God's grace means
that our weaknesses are perfectly covered by God's forgiveness of
our past and God's empowerment of our future.

"My power is made perfect in weakness" does not mean that God is
not perfectly powerful to begin with. It simply means that His power
becomes more *obvious to people* when it is shown in spite of the
human weakness of the person He uses as His instrument. But for

God to use us in this way, we have to make a decision: Do we really *want* to show the power of God and have people give glory to Him, or are we deep down seeking glory for ourselves? If the latter is our true motivation, then our weaknesses will continue to grate against us. But if the former is our motivation, then our weaknesses may even help us reach our goal.

Some Contemporary Examples

A contemporary example of how God's strength can be seen in human weakness is <u>Joni Eareckson Tada</u>, the artist and author who became a quadriplegic through a diving accident when she was a teenager. At first she thought her life had ended with the accident, but God showed her how to make beautiful art by holding a brush in her teeth. And even more, He showed her how His love could give her a reason to live. What she has written about her life has inspired millions.

Looking at a different kind of weakness, <u>Chuck Colson</u> once had great power from a human perspective. He was one of the most influential people in Nixon's White House. But God brought him down. The Watergate scandal put him in jail and took away all of his power. But that was when, in his weakness, God came to him, saved him, and gave him a heart for prison ministry. His ministry and writing have also touched millions.

Paul's Motivation

That Paul's true motivation was to honor and focus attention on God is why he could say as he does in verse 10, "I delight in weakness," and "when I am weak, then I am strong." Paul knew that he had no true strength unless it was the strength of God working through him. There had been a time when he had relied on his own strength and that strength had failed him. Only when he became at peace with his weaknesses and relied on God's strength did God start using him in a way that made him one of the great religious figures of history.

Implications for Our Witness

If it is okay to have weaknesses, since we rely on God's strength, what does that mean for how we witness (tell others about Jesus)? <u>It means first and foremost that our witness should never point to us but always to God</u>. We should not say, "Be a perfect saint like me," but rather, "Let God save and set you apart for His purposes, as he has done for millions of struggling sinners throughout history." We should not be saying, "Follow me," but rather, "Follow Christ: He is the Way." We should not be saying, "I have reached all of my spiritual goals," but rather, "I am on a journey toward being more Christlike—why not join me on the way?!"

Who are some contemporary people that the leader referred to as examples of how God's power is made perfect in weakness? Can you think of others?

What two implications of what Paul says about weakness are there for your witness?

today's session (cont'd)

<u>Another important implication for our witness is that we need to see admitting our weakness as a tool of our witness rather than a possible stumbling block.</u> Some people reason, "If people see my weaknesses, then they might not think I am a true Christian and it will hurt my witness." <u>There are two things wrong with this reasoning: (1) people who know us probably already know our weaknesses more than we think—sometimes they are just too polite to tell us they know!; and (2) people *know* that they have weaknesses, and they want to know what to do about them.</u> People who pretend they have no weaknesses can offer others no help. Only people who admit their weaknesses and point to the One who is helping them with those weaknesses can offer hope.

What problems are there with reasoning, "If people see my weakness, then they might not think I am a true Christian and it will hurt my witness"?

Witnessing should always begin with sharing who we really are and what we have really struggled with in our spiritual journey. This involves a certain vulnerability on our part. We may be afraid that people will think less of us. We may be afraid that people will put us down or take advantage of whatever weakness we reveal. But when we have these fears, we need to remember the lesson Paul learned and shared in this text: "When I am weak, then I am strong." Only when we take that lesson seriously can we truly witness to the life-changing power of Jesus Christ.

notes:

✚

⟲ Remain in groups of 6–8 people, in a horseshoe configuration.

In this small-group session, students will be applying the lessons of the text to their own lives through the following questions.

The students were asked (in the student book) to choose an answer for each question and explain why.

Share with the class the following thoughts on how the lessons of this text might be applied today. The answers to the student book questions (provided in the margin) are underlined unless the question requires a personal answer.

What are some ways you can learn about your weaknesses?

Why is submitting your weaknesses to God a vital step?

Learning from the Story (5-7 minutes)

1. What would be your closest equivalent to Paul's "thorn in the flesh"—a weakness (physical, emotional, or spiritual) that you have tried to get rid of but haven't been able to so far?

2. What would you say is the best way to deal with a personal weakness?

   ☐ hide it   ☐ work constantly at overcoming it
   ☐ be honest about it   ☐ submit it to the Lord
   ☐ other: _____

3. When has God shown His power by using you in spite of your weakness?

life change lessons (5-7 minutes)

It's easy to talk about being vulnerable and sharing our weaknesses, but it's harder to actually do it. Here are some things you can do to start:

1. LEARN WHAT OTHERS SEE AS YOUR WEAKNESSES. <u>This can be done by: (a) making a list of things people have criticized about you recently; (b) asking a couple of your closest, most trusted friends what they see as your weaknesses; (c) listing three times that you feel you failed someone, and then next to each one writing down the personal quality you have that contributed to the failures. Compare these lists.</u>

2. SCHEDULE AN APPOINTMENT WITH GOD WHERE YOU SUBMIT YOUR WEAKNESSES TO HIM AND PRAY THAT HE WILL SHOW HIS STRENGTH THROUGH THEM. This is a vital step! <u>If you just list your weaknesses, it will depress you. But if you ask God to use them, others will see His strength and power.</u> Remember what God did through Paul!

3. SHARE YOUR WEAKNESSES WITH A CLOSE FRIEND OR IN A SMALL GROUP OF BELIEVERS THIS WEEK. This will help you look at and come to peace with who you truly are. Ask this friend or group to join you in prayer that God will show His strength through you in spite of these weaknesses.

◡ CARING TIME
Remain in groups of 6–8 people, in a horseshoe configuration.

Hand out the Prayer/ Praise Report to the entire group. Ask each subgroup to pray for the empty chair. Pray specifically for God to guide you to someone to bring next week to fill that chair.

After a sufficient time of prayer in subgroups, close in a corporate prayer. Say, "Next week we will talk about: 'Becoming An Authentic Christian.' "

Remind participants of the daily Scripture readings and reflective questions found on page 28.

Caring Time   (15-20 minutes)

Take time now to pray for one another and for your own special concerns. Remember the "thorns" that people mentioned ("Learning from the Story," question 1). Ask that God would speak to each group member about his or her weaknesses, as He did with Paul. Also, remember to pray about the concerns listed on the Prayer/Praise Report.

Close by thanking God for bringing you together as a group and by asking Him to help each group member grow spiritually.

notes:

BIBLE STUDY NOTES

Reference Notes

Use these notes to gain further understanding
of the text as you study on your own.

2 CORINTHIANS 12:6
speak the truth

speaking the truth. This may infer that Paul's opponents had fabricated tales of their visions.

think more of me than is warranted. Apostolic authority is seen, not by a person's mystical experiences, but in the way a person lives and by the message the person preaches.

2 CORINTHIANS 12:7
conceit

To keep me from becoming conceited. In fact, so wonderful were the visions Paul had been having that Paul needed to be brought back to earth via a very troubling physical condition.

a thorn in my flesh. It is unknown what Paul means here. Two viable options are: (1) a chronic physical ailment; or (2) the continual opposition Paul encountered. Speculation in the area of physical ailments has focused on a vision problem Paul may have had (see Gal. 4:15), or maybe

**2 CORINTHIANS 12:7
(cont'd)**

a problem with seizures. It is significant that Paul generally used someone to write his letters (see for instance Romans 16:22), and when he did write with his own hand he mentioned the "large letters" with which he wrote (see Gal. 6:11).

messenger of Satan. Sickness was thought to be caused by Satan, but the false apostles in Corinth are also referred to as servants of Satan (2 Cor. 11:13–15).

torment me. Literally, "to continually torment me." Whatever the problem was, it was chronic, though not debilitating.

2 CORINTHIANS 12:8

Three times. There are parallels between Paul's experience and that of Jesus in the Garden of Gethsemane. Like Jesus, Paul was not delivered from the hardship that faced him; rather, he received strength to remain faithful in the midst of suffering.

the Lord. This is the only explicit reference in the New Testament to prayer made directly to Christ rather than to God.

**2 CORINTHIANS 12:9
*grace and power***

This sentence is the lens through which all of 2 Corinthians must be understood as it reflects the fundamental misunderstanding that both the false teachers and the Corinthians had about the gospel. They thought that the power of God meant that Christians should escape or avoid the experiences of weakness, vulnerability, suffering, and hardship that are common to life. Paul's emphasis throughout the letter has been that the power of God does not mean such trials are avoided, but that God empowers believers to love, to bring healing, to serve, and to be faithful in the midst of such times (see 2 Cor. 1:3–11). Thus, the Christian life follows the pattern of the cross in which the glory of God was revealed through the suffering of Jesus on behalf of the world.

**2 CORINTHIANS 12:10
*source of strength***

when I am weak, then I am strong. In asserting that his weakness made it possible for God to show His strength in him, Paul aligned himself with a perspective also voiced in the Old Testament. Gideon was told to make his army *smaller* so that people would not think their natural strength brought them the victory and would give glory to God in *His* strength (see Judg. 7).

notes:

Session

3

Becoming an
Authentic Christian

Prepare for the Session

	READINGS	REFLECTIVE QUESTIONS
Monday	Acts 5:1–2	What part of your life do you keep back from God?
Tuesday	Acts 5:3–4	How do you handle confrontation?
Wednesday	Acts 5:5–6	When have you experienced a godly fear?
Thursday	Acts 5:7–9	When have you feared men over God? Why?
Friday	Acts 5:10–11	What event has God used to get your attention?
Saturday	Acts 5:10	How important is it for you to be an authentic Christian?
Sunday	Acts 5:11	How would you respond to those struggling with hypocrisy in your church?

notes:

OUR GOALS FOR
THIS SESSION ARE:

In groups of 6–8,
gather people in
a horseshoe
configuration.

Make sure everyone
has a name tag.

Take time to share
information on class
parties that are coming
up as well as any
relevant church events.

INTRODUCE THE
ICEBREAKER ACTIVITY:
The students have
been given instructions
in their books.

After the Icebreaker
say something like,
"Today we will be
talking about a
couple who got
caught 'red-handed' in
an act of deception.
We will be considering
what their story says
to us (by negative
example) about
what it means to be
authentic Christians."

Hand out the
Prayer/Praise Report.
A sample copy is
on pages 158-159.
Have people write
down prayer requests
and praises. Then
have the prayer
coordinator collect
the report and make
copies for use during
the Caring Time.

BIBLE STUDY

- to learn what the story of Ananias and Sapphira has to say about being an authentic Christian
- to discover the qualities of an authentic Christian
- to look specifically at how to avoid hypocrisy in our Christian lives

LIFE CHANGE

- to find a spiritual advisor
- to read Scripture daily, remembering to apply it to ourselves
- to encourage Christian friends to give us both supportive and developmental feedback

3

Icebreaker   (10-15 minutes)

Caught Red-Handed. Have each person answer both questions before going on to the next person.

1. In which of the following areas of behavior did your parents catch you red-handed when you were a child or adolescent?

   ☐ skipping school
   ☐ smoking
   ☐ playing doctor
   ☐ looking at sexually-oriented material
   ☐ lying about where I was
   ☐ other:_____

2. What did your parents do and how did it affect you?

notes:

**LEARNING FROM
THE BIBLE**

ACTS 5:1–11

**Have a member of
the class, selected
ahead of time,
read the passage
from Acts.**

Bible Study   (30-45 minutes)

The Scripture for this week:

¹*Now a man named Ananias, together with his wife Sapphira,
also sold a piece of property.* ²*With his wife's full knowledge he kept
back part of the money for himself, but brought the rest and put it at
the apostles' feet.*

³*Then Peter said, "Ananias, how is it that Satan has so filled your
heart that you have lied to the Holy Spirit and have kept for yourself
some of the money you received for the land?* ⁴*Didn't it belong to you
before it was sold? And after it was sold, wasn't the money at your
disposal? What made you think of doing such a thing? You have not
lied to men but to God."*

⁵*When Ananias heard this, he fell down and died. And great fear
seized all who heard what had happened.* ⁶*Then the young men came
forward, wrapped up his body, and carried him out and buried him.*

⁷*About three hours later his wife came in, not knowing what had
happened.* ⁸*Peter asked her, "Tell me, is this the price you and Ananias
got for the land?" "Yes," she said, "that is the price."*

⁹*Peter said to her, "How could you agree to test the Spirit of the
Lord? Look! The feet of the men who buried your husband are at the
door, and they will carry you out also."*

¹⁰*At that moment she fell down at his feet and died. Then the
young men came in and, finding her dead, carried her out and buried
her beside her husband.* ¹¹*Great fear seized the whole church and all
who heard about these events.*

notes:

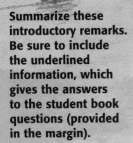

Summarize these introductory remarks. Be sure to include the underlined information, which gives the answers to the student book questions (provided in the margin).

What examples of artificial things in our society are referred to in the presentation? What additional examples can you think of?

What examples can you think of where someone was an "artificial Christian"?

...about today's session (5 minutes)

WHAT IS REAL?

We live in a society in which so much is artificial. <u>What looks like wood in many of our new homes is not wood at all, but rather vinyl or some other artificial laminate. What looks like a brick or natural stone building is often just a brick or stone facade</u>. Many of us do the same with our bodies. Men have hair sewn on their heads when they are going bald. Women and men have <u>plastic surgery</u> done on their faces to make them more attractive. <u>Artificial sweeteners</u> are in many of our drinks, and, in fact, just about every product we buy has some artificial ingredient to make it appear like something else. Some of them are stronger or better than the real thing.

3

KEEP IT REAL

While in any given case arguments can be made that many of these artificial things are good, one thing our world definitely does *not* need is artificial Christians. We do have them, of course. They act pious in church, while during the week they are involved in activities so sinful that nobody would ever suspect them of being Christians. They say all the right words about Christ and the church, but when you turn your back on them, you suddenly discover a knife in it!

However, what we seek to do in this session is not warn about *other* people being artificial Christians, but to warn those attending this group against becoming one themselves. In a society that judges by appearance and in which much is artificial, it's easy to think that what counts is how things look. "Image is everything!" But in the kingdom of God, where God decides what is important and what is not, that is not what counts. God is one who sees beyond facades to the heart, and He likes the real thing.

In this session we will look at a passage where a couple of Christians tried being artificial. They quickly learned that God does not tolerate such behavior. Perhaps through their negative example we can learn what it means to be an authentic Christian.

notes:

⊕

Remain in groups of 6–8 people, in a horseshoe configuration.

In this small-group session, students will be responding to the following questions that will help them share their stories in terms of the story of Ananias and Sapphira.

Have the students explore these questions together.

Identifying with the Story (5-7 minutes)

1. When is the last time you remember being called on the carpet for something you did wrong or someone thought you did wrong?

2. How do you most often react when you are called on the carpet for something?

   ☐ I act guilty—whether I am or not.
   ☐ If I'm guilty, I can't hide it.
   ☐ I feel like a little kid.
   ☐ I get defensive, even if I'm wrong.
   ☐ I charm or talk my way out of it.
   ☐ I get angry and blow up.
   ☐ Other: _____

3. Had you been Ananias or Sapphira, and had you done what they did, what are the chances you would have tried the same cover-up and met the same fate?

   ☐ No way!
   ☐ A fair chance—I HAVE tried that approach before.
   ☐ A strong chance—I hate to admit when I have done something wrong.
   ☐ It's almost certain I would have been TOAST!

notes:

Share with your class the following information which you may modify according to your own perspectives and teaching needs. The answers to the student book questions (provided in the margin) are underlined.

today's session (15-20 minutes)

There are times when we idealize the early church. We talk of all the great miracles they did or we envy them for their intense sense of community and caring (Acts 2:42–47; 4:32–37). However, whenever we are tempted to feel that way, we might look at the story of Ananias and Sapphira. Preachers looking for texts upon which to preach often avoid this one. On one hand, it's the story of one of the great scandals of the early church; on the other hand, it is the story of a punishment that many find harsh and excessive. It is nonetheless true that sometimes we learn from negative examples, and the scriptural stories we avoid can often surprise us with new insights we can't get from the texts we have examined a thousand times. Let's see what this story can teach us about being an authentic Christian.

Background to the Story

To understand the story, we have to know some background from the previous chapter. The church at this time did have a very intense and caring fellowship. They not only met and studied together frequently, but they also shared meals and pooled their financial resources, selling their belongings and <u>using the proceeds for those who were in need</u>. Ananias and Sapphira wanted it to look like they were doing this. However, they hedged and decided to reserve a portion of the money from the sale of their property for themselves while saying that they gave the full amount.

How was the Christian church using the proceeds of property that was sold and donated by members?

What happened to Ananias and Sapphira? Were they greedy? Did they seek unwarranted praise? God doesn't tell us why they lied to the Holy Spirit, only the severity of the sin. The sentence of death imposed by God may seem harsh in today's "tolerant" society, but it should speak volumes about God's view of sin.

Putting What Happened Into Perspective

We also need to see what happened in relationship to the unique situation of the early church. The church was just getting started. People were looking at these Christians closely and asking questions like, "Can we trust these people?" "Is this movement of God?" and "Are these people authentically living out what they are teaching?" In relationship to the question, "Is this movement of God?" the judgment on Ananias and Sapphira would certainly have sent forth a message that God's power was with this group of believers. That is the importance of the final sentence, "Great fear seized the whole church and all who heard about these events." They were not afraid that the same thing might happen to them. Rather, this fear that filled the church was a reverence or awe for the power of God.

today's session (cont'd)

The questions people were raising concerning the early church's trustworthiness and authenticity are particularly important. Nothing destroys a religious movement quicker than hypocrisy. In our time we can think of the effect of the falls of such well-known figures as Jimmy Swaggart and Jim and Tammy Bakker. At the susceptible time in history in which the early church found itself, *any* sign of hypocrisy had to be dealt with swiftly and surely.

Approaches to Eliminating Hypocrisy

God certainly does not execute hypocrites today. If He did, people would probably be dropping like flies! But this story underscores the importance of authenticity in the life of the church and in the lives of Christians. We have to be the kind of Christians we say we are. How do we do that? Let's look at the approaches people try.

Some people try the *aim low approach*. The reasoning behind this is that if you keep your standards low enough, it's much easier to hit those standards and you won't be considered a hypocrite. In marriage, the promise has changed from staying together "as long as you both shall live" to "as long as you both shall love." That's an easier standard to reach. Often in politics it's don't be honest, but rather maintain "plausible deniability." It's what people expect you to do anyway. The "aim low approach" may eliminate hypocrisy, but it does so by destroying the values on which a healthy society is based.

A variation of the "aim low approach" is the *live and let live approach*. The most important part of this approach is to never say or even imply anything is wrong in the behavior of another person. If you do, you are being "judgmental" and if there are any flaws in what you are doing, then you are a hypocrite for pointing out what the other person did wrong. Didn't Jesus say, " 'Do not judge, or you too will be judged' " (Matt. 7:1)? However, there is a difference between judgmentalism and confronting wrong behavior. Jesus confronted wrong behavior all the time. So what is the difference? Judgmentalism is when we criticize while being blind to our own shortcomings. When we do that, we are being hypocritical. However, what kind of society would we be if we could never question wrong behavior? We couldn't confront those who are being racists. We would have to tolerate those dealing drugs to our children.

A healthier way to avoid hypocrisy is *spiritual honesty*. This includes being open about our own shortcomings. We confess we are sinners and never pretend that the sins we commit are less wrong and more pure than the sins of everyone else. When we confront others with what they are doing wrong, we do so only after prayerful

What examples are given of how hypocrisy has hurt the church in modern times?

What three approaches to dealing with hypocrisy are discussed?

What problems are presented by the "aim low" and "live and let live" approaches?

How does spiritual honesty help us avoid hypocrisy?

We should confront others with what they are doing wrong only after _____.

self-examination, and we give them the right to confront us in a similar way if they see us doing something wrong. We don't present ourselves as better than we are—or better than the other person. We confess we do wrong and at the same time we constantly try to reach higher moral and spiritual ground.

Every era will have its people like Ananias and Sapphira. But if we have more and more Christians reaching for spiritual honesty, our witness will survive their falls, and God will bless the faithful witness of His children.

notes:

3

✝

U Remain in groups of 6–8 people, in a horseshoe configuration.

In this small-group session, students will be applying the lessons of the text to their own lives through the following questions.

The students were asked (in the student book) to choose an answer for each question and explain why.

Learning from the Story (5-7 minutes)

1. How do you react emotionally to this story?

   ☐ shocked—that God and the disciples would have been so harsh.

   ☐ scared—maybe God would do the same to me!

   ☐ unsympathetic—Ananias and Sapphira had it coming!

   ☐ only somewhat sympathetic—it was a hard judgment, but a necessary one

   ☐ confused—I'm sure there was a reason for what happened, but I don't get it.

   ☐ other: _____

2. What do you think might have happened had God simply let this deception slide?

   ☐ Nobody would have known the difference.

   ☐ It would have encouraged more deception and hypocrisy in the church.

   ☐ It would have shown God's forgiving nature.

   ☐ It would have made people think that Christians were no different than anyone else.

   ☐ other:_____

3. When have *you* felt tempted to make it appear that you were being more loving or sacrificial than you really were? What did you end up doing and how did you feel about it?

life change lessons (5-7 minutes)

The church will probably always have hypocrites, at least until Christ returns. But each of us has a choice about what we do in response to that reality. What concrete things can we do so that we are part of the solution of Christian authenticity instead of part of the problem of hypocrisy? Here are some specific actions we can do.

1. FIND A PERSON TO BE YOUR SPIRITUAL ADVISOR. This should be a mature Christian of the same sex whom you trust. You should be able to confess your sins to this person in the spirit of <u>James 5:16</u>. Do this not because you have to or because you believe a human being has to grant you forgiveness. Do it because it helps you become accountable to another person and because God's forgiveness can best be felt through another human being. <u>When you confess to another human being, you realize that another person knows you exactly as you are, and this reduces the temptation to be false.</u> This person can also help you direct your spiritual growth by suggesting various spiritual disciplines or devotional readings that will help you.

2. READ SCRIPTURE DAILY, REMEMBERING TO APPLY IT TO YOURSELF. Each time you read Scripture, let it speak to you—not your spouse, your neighbor, or your coworker. Ask yourself the question: In what way does this challenge me to behave differently?

3. ENCOURAGE CHRISTIAN FRIENDS TO GIVE YOU BOTH SUPPORTIVE AND DEVELOPMENTAL FEEDBACK. We all need affirmation to grow, and that is good. We also need our Christian friends to be able to say how they really see us. If this is done with caring and confidentiality, we can use this feedback to become more authentic Christians.

Caring Time (15-20 minutes)

Take time now to pray for one another and for your own special concerns. Remember the "thorns" that people mentioned ("Learning from the Story," question 1). Ask that God would speak to each group member about his or her weaknesses, as He did with Paul. Also, remember to pray about the concerns listed on the Prayer/Praise Report.

Close by thanking God for bringing you together as a group and by asking Him to help each group member grow spiritually.

Share with the class the following thoughts on how the lessons of this text might be applied today. The answers to the student book questions (provided in the margin) are underlined unless the question requires a personal answer.

What Bible passage advises us to confess our sins to one another?

Why does confessing to another human reduce the temptation to be false?

☾ CARING TIME
Remain in groups of 6–8 people, in a horseshoe configuration.

Hand out the Prayer/Praise Report to the entire group. Ask each subgroup to pray for the empty chair. Pray specifically for God to guide you to someone to bring next week to fill that chair.

After a sufficient time of prayer in subgroups, close in a corporate prayer. Say, "Next week we will talk about: 'My Life As a Witness.'"

Remind participants of the daily Scripture readings and reflective questions found on page 38.

Reference Notes

Use these notes to gain further understanding
of the text as you study on your own.

ACTS 5:1–11
hypocrisy

The hypocrisy of Ananias and Sapphira stands in stark contrast to the upbeat, positive picture of the early church presented so far. This action threatened the trust and integrity that formed the basis of the fellowship among the believers.

ACTS 5:2
booty

he kept back. This rare Greek word is used in the Septuagint version of Joshua 7:1 to describe Achan's sin of taking part of the booty from Jericho that was to be devoted to God. Luke may be using this word to make a connection between Achan's sin and that of Ananias.

ACTS 5:4
lying to God

You have not lied to men but to God. Peter's statement is not to minimize the fact that they *did* lie to people, but to highlight the fact that this lie was primarily an affront to God. Their lie showed that they failed to take the Holy Spirit's presence with the community seriously.

ACTS 5:5–10
sin's consequence

Many today find this incident disturbing. However, it does need to be seen in light of the fact that trust was vital to this early Christian community. Those who were not true to their word threatened Christianity's witness. The surprise exposure of their sin and the direct act of God caused both Ananias and Sapphira to die.

ACTS 5:9
a test

test the Spirit of the Lord. Their act betrayed their disbelief that God's Spirit really knew all that happened (Ex. 17:2; Deut. 6:16; Ps. 139:1–7). This verse shows how completely the early Christians identified God (v. 4) with the Spirit (v. 3) and with (the Lord) Jesus (v. 9).

ACTS 5:11
awe

The result of this incident was that the entire community recognized the seriousness of the presence of God in their midst (Heb. 10:31; 12:28–29). *Great fear.* The early Christians were not afraid of being similarly struck down by God, but rather this should be more properly understood as, "they felt a great sense of awe at the power of God."

church. This is the first use of the word *ekklesia* in Acts. Although the English versions of the Old Testament do not reflect it, this word, along with *synagogue*, was commonly used in the Septuagint to translate the Hebrew word *qahal* referring to the assembly of God's people. Since *synagogue* became the name for the Jewish places of worship (the synagogue), the Christians used *ekklesia* to refer to themselves. By so doing, they claimed a common Old Testament term to identify themselves as the true Israel of God.

notes:

Session

4

My Life As a Witness

Prepare for the Session

	READINGS	REFLECTIVE QUESTIONS
Monday	Matthew 5:13	Who influenced you to follow Christ?
Tuesday	Matthew 5:13	How is your life a preservative of the good news about Jesus?
Wednesday	Matthew 5:13	What in your life could hinder you from being an effective witness?
Thursday	Matthew 5:14	How does your life shine in your relationship with God?
Friday	Matthew 5:15	What causes you to be ashamed of the gospel?
Saturday	Matthew 5:16	How can you let your "light" shine?
Sunday	Matthew 5:16	Who would you like to bring with you to heaven?

notes:

✝ BIBLE STUDY

OUR GOALS FOR THIS SESSION ARE:

♆ **In groups of 6–8, gather people in a horseshoe configuration.**

Make sure everyone has a name tag.

Take time to share information on class parties that are coming up as well as any relevant church events.

INTRODUCE THE ICEBREAKER ACTIVITY: The students have been given instructions in their books.

After the Icebreaker say something like, "Not all of us give off light in the same way. But if we are in Christ, we should give light to those around us. How we do that will be our focus today."

Hand out the Prayer/Praise Report. A sample copy is on pages 158-159. Have people write down prayer requests and praises. Then have the prayer coordinator collect the report and make copies for use during the Caring Time.

BIBLE STUDY
- to consider what Jesus meant when He said we were to be the "salt of the earth" and the "light of the world"
- to understand why living our lives as witnesses, persons who tell others about Jesus, doesn't mean we have to be perfect
- to consider why what we do speaks louder than what we say

LIFE CHANGE
- to pray that you will live a Christlike life
- to list two or three behaviors you think are hurting your witness
- to get involved in one ministry where you can put love into action on a regular basis

4

Icebreaker (10-15 minutes)

The Light We Shine. What kind of light best describes each of the members in your group? For each of the lights below, choose a group member who best fits that category. Share these with each other in a spirit of affirmation.

CAMPFIRE LIGHT: You give warmth and light to a cold night.

FLASHLIGHT: You direct light to the especially dark areas where it is needed most.

100-WATT BULB: Your personality lights up the room!

FIREPLACE LIGHT: You bring people together around your crackling warmth.

MOONLIGHT: You reflect well the light of the Son.

SUNLIGHT: You are a natural light that gives life to those around you.

NEON LIGHT: Your light brings personality, flash, and color to the group.

notes:

Bible Study (30-45 minutes)

The Scripture for this week:

¹³"You are the salt of the earth. But if the salt loses its saltiness, how can it be made salty again? It is no longer good for anything, except to be thrown out and trampled by men.

¹⁴"You are the light of the world. A city on a hill cannot be hidden. ¹⁵Neither do people light a lamp and put it under a bowl. Instead they put it on its stand, and it gives light to everyone in the house. ¹⁶In the same way, let your light shine before men, that they may see your good deeds and praise your Father in heaven."

notes:

...about today's session (5 minutes)

WHO IS WATCHING ME?

It has been said, "You are the only Bible your neighbor may ever read." That means people who don't read the Bible may get an idea of who God is and what a difference God can make by observing the behavior of Christians. That makes how we live our lives a rather awesome responsibility and, for some, an intimidating one. Some of us might say, "Since I cannot be perfect, what happens when non-Christians are watching when I stumble? Does it mean that my witness has been destroyed?"

Whether we see living our witness as an awesome and exciting challenge or as a frightening and intimidating expectation, it is a reality nonetheless. Once people know we claim to be Christians or even that we go to church regularly, they will be watching. Some will watch hoping to find a viable alternative to their lifestyle, and some will watch so they can debunk us and validate their lifestyle. Either way, they will be watching. How will we react to being observed in this way?

MY LIFE AS A WITNESS

In this session we will look at what it means that our lives are a witness. We will consider what it means when we fall, and how to maintain our witness in the midst of our imperfections. We will take a look at what it means that Christ is within us, empowering us to live as He would have us live, and how that helps us do what we could not do on our own. Above all, we will seek to remember what it means that in all we do we should seek to honor and focus attention on God, not ourselves. That is the essence of what it means to live for Jesus Christ.

What did the leader say is the essence of what it means to live for Jesus Christ?

notes:

4

◑ Remain in groups of 6–8 people, in a horseshoe configuration.

In this small-group session, students will be responding to the following questions that will help them share their stories in terms of Jesus' teaching about salt and light.

Have the students explore these questions together.

Identifying with the Story (5-7 minutes)

1. When it comes to flavoring the food you eat, are you more into:

   hot and spicy. . . . . mild and subtle

   ketchup and   let the natural
   steak sauce. . . . . flavors come through

   lots of salt and butter   air pop it and
   on popcorn· leave it plain

2. According to your natural personality, which are you more likely to do?

   . . . .
   1   2   3   4   5   6   7   8   9   10
   I shine my light from   I hide my light under a bowl,
   the hill for all to see!   and hope no one finds me!

3. If you could have a spotlight put on just one thing you have done in the past month, what would it be?

Share with your class the following information which you may modify according to your own perspectives and teaching needs. The answers to the student book questions (provided in the margin) are underlined.

today's session (15-20 minutes)

There are perils to a salt-free diet. No, I'm not going against modern medical opinion. It is true that Americans get far too much salt and that it is a contributing factor in high blood pressure. Still, salt is important. It is vital to help the body maintain a proper balance of fluids. The average adult needs 1/2 to 1 1/2 teaspoons of salt a day, which can normally be found in the food we eat. When I talk of the perils of a salt-free diet, however, I'm not talking about the salt we eat. I'm talking about the salt of the world. I'm talking about what Christians are supposed to be.

The Importance of Salt

Christ says that those of us who are Christians should be the salt of the earth. What does that mean? Some Christians seem to interpret it to mean that we are to go around giving each other high blood pressure! That's not what Jesus intended! <u>In ancient times, salt was indispensable in preserving food, especially in hot areas like Israel. As a result, it had great value.</u> At various times a bag of salt was deemed as precious as a man's life. In Greece, slaves were bought and sold with salt. This is probably how the saying originated, "not worth his salt." The term "salary" is also derived from salt, and refers to a time when in Rome soldiers were paid money to buy their ration of salt. Salt was highly prized in the ancient world, largely because of its value in preserving food.

Why was salt so valuable in ancient times?

Just as salt was valued because it could preserve food and keep it from spoiling, so the Christian should act as a preservative in society to keep it from "spoiling." And societies can spoil. They can spoil by letting the values that are essential to the society be sacrificed to greed, lust, and expediency. We see some of that spoiling in our country today. We see it in the rise of youth violence, the drive-by shootings, the increased use of dangerous drugs. We see it in our business world, with insider trading scandals and unethical business practices. We see it in our advertising and movie industries, where sex and violence are used to sell.

We act as "salt" whenever we, through how we act or speak, influence the world around us for Jesus Christ. While the speaking part of this is important, it is especially important that we act out our witness. In verse 16, Jesus says, " 'let your light shine before men, that they may see your *good deeds* and praise your Father in heaven' " (italics added).

Inappropriate Reactions

What are two inappropriate ways to react to Jesus' words that we are to be "salt" and "light" in the world?

There are a couple of inappropriate ways to react to this command that we need to look at before we consider our response to it. <u>One inappropriate reaction is to become intimidated by it</u>. We think it means that we have to be perfect, and we know that we aren't. We're afraid that people will see our imperfections and that will be a poor witness. However, we must realize that what people need in this world is a model of how to react to human imperfection. Others know they are imperfect also. Do they simply give in to their imperfections, living their life by the lowest moral standard possible so they don't ever fall short? Or do they hide their imperfections so it *appears* they have none? <u>The Christian way is to point to Jesus Christ as the One who brings us grace and forgiveness in the midst of our imperfection</u>. We need to model an attitude that says, "Yes, I mess up, but God forgives me because of what Jesus did! Yes, I'm not all that I should be, but Christ empowers me to be oh so much more than I was. So, be patient, God's not finished with me!"

How should a Christian deal with his or her imperfections?

4

<u>We should also avoid the other inappropriate reaction: Pretending that we are perfect in all we do</u>. Most people recognize this as phony and unattainable. They also resent it because such people generally end up judging the shortcomings of others. For some people, the "salt" they provide is salt that is rubbed into the wounds of the struggling—people on the street who have not been able to make it in our world; people whose marital dreams have fallen in divorce; teenagers who have had trouble finding their way. That self-righteous kind of "salt" is not the kind we are called upon to provide to the world.

Living as Salt and Light

If we truly want to be a light in the world, what light should we reflect?

What we *should* do is always seek to help other people see Christ through our actions. The second part of our passage talks about being a "light" before people. <u>The best way we can do that is by reflecting the purest light of all, Jesus Christ.</u> Jesus said, " 'I am the light of the world' " (John 8:12), and like the moon reflects the *sun*, we are to reflect the *Son*. How this works is shown by combining two Scripture references, one from John's gospel and one from the letter of 1 John. <u>John 1:18</u> tells us that even though "No one has ever seen God," Jesus has made Him known to us. <u>First John 4:12</u> takes this a step further when it says, "No one has ever seen God; but if we love one another, God lives in us." <u>If we let Christ's love shine through us like a light, we complete the chain: The unseen God is revealed in Christ, who in turn is revealed in us.</u>

What two passages, both written by John, start with the phrase, "No one has ever seen God"? How is their meaning connected?

What would you say to someone who thinks that to be "salt" and "light" in the world, a person has to be perfect?

Again, we don't have to be perfect to do this. <u>Think of the people who have shown Christ's light to you. They weren't perfect. But they nevertheless let the light of Jesus Christ shine through them.</u> Or we

today's session (cont'd)

can think of those who shed a wider light in the world: Mother Teresa, Martin Luther King, Jr. or Billy Graham. All of them showed and admitted their imperfection. But how many millions have been affected by the light of Jesus Christ reflected in these three people? Most of us will not affect as many as any of these. Our assignment, rather, is to be "salt" and "light" to those in our immediate world— to our family members, coworkers, and neighbors. If Christians would just do that, how this world would change!

notes:

Remain in groups of 6–8 people, in a horseshoe configuration.

In this small-group session, students will be applying the lessons of the text to their own lives through the following questions.

The students were asked (in the student book) to choose an answer for each question and explain why.

Learning from the Story (5-7 minutes)

1. How do you feel about the idea of "letting your light shine" before people so they can "see your good deeds" and "praise God"?

   ☐ It sounds like thinly veiled egotism.
   ☐ It sounds scary—what if I fall on my face?
   ☐ It's the kind of challenge I need.
   ☐ If God helps me, perhaps I can do it.
   ☐ other: _____

2. Who, by the way he or she lived, shed light on *you* in your formative years?

3. In order to take this passage seriously, what is the first thing you need to do?

   ☐ overcome my natural shyness
   ☐ pray for God's strength for my weaknesses
   ☐ free up some time to get involved in some caring ministries
   ☐ conquer an enslaving habit that is making me a poor witness
   ☐ other: _____

life change lessons (5-7 minutes)

What needs to happen in your life for this session to be a success?

_____ **is the _____ within you that makes the light shine forth.**

All of us could come away from today's session with an interesting array of facts and insights to impress people: Where the word *salary* came from; what it means that a person isn't "worth his salt"; the connection between two Bible passages that start with the phrase, "No one has ever seen God." If such things are all we come away with after having been here, then this time together will have been a failure. <u>We must come away with an action plan to make our lives a preserving salt in a decaying society and a light to a dark world</u>. Here are some things we ought to do in order to head in that direction.

1. PRAY THAT YOU WILL LIVE A CHRISTLIKE LIFE. If you remain at the center of your life and what you do with that life, you will never be a light to anyone. The best you can ever be is what many of our households have too many of already: flashlights without working batteries. <u>Christ</u> is the "<u>battery</u>" within you that makes the light shine forth. That's how the apostle Paul kept his life going as he said, "I no longer live, but Christ lives in me" (Gal. 2:20).

2. LIST TWO OR THREE BEHAVIORS THAT YOU THINK ARE HURTING YOUR WITNESS. This helps get them "on the table" where you can pray about them and start working on overcoming them. Have a caring, trusted friend help you develop this list.

3. GET INVOLVED IN ONE OF THE MINISTRIES OF THE CHURCH WHERE YOU PUT LOVE INTO ACTION ON A REGULAR BASIS. It's not enough to just avoid things that have a negative effect on your witness. People rarely refer to someone as a "light" in their life because of all the wrong or irritating things they did not do. They talk about acts of sincere love and sacrifice. This should be a ministry that is a passion for you and for which you have a gift or talent to contribute.

4

notes:

⊌ CARING TIME
Remain in groups of 6–8 people, in a horseshoe configuration.

Hand out the Prayer/ Praise Report to the entire group. Ask each subgroup to pray for the empty chair. Pray specifically for God to guide you to someone to bring next week to fill that chair.

After a sufficient time of prayer in subgroups, close in a corporate prayer. Say, "Next week we will talk about: 'Spiritual Disciplines in My Life.' "

Remind participants of the daily Scripture readings and reflective questions found on page 48.

Caring Time   (15-20 minutes)

Close by taking time to pray for one another and for your own special concerns. Thank God for the person(s) mentioned in question 2 of "Learning from the Story." Ask for strength to make whatever life changes people need in order to strengthen their witness. Also, use the Prayer/Praise Report and pray for the concerns listed.

Conclude your prayer time by reading Psalm 139:1–4,23–24 together:

> *O Lord, you have searched me and you know me.*
> *You know when I sit and when I rise;*
> *you perceive my thoughts from afar.*
> *You discern my going out and my lying down;*
> *you are familiar with all my ways.*
> *Before a word is on my tongue*
> *you know it completely, O Lord.*
>
> *Search me, O God, and know my heart;*
> *test me and know my anxious thoughts.*
> *See if there is any offensive way in me,*
> *and lead me in the way everlasting.*

notes:

BIBLE STUDY NOTES

Reference Notes

Use these notes to gain further understanding
of the text as you study on your own.

MATTHEW 5:13
valuable commodity

salt. Salt was a very valuable commodity in ancient times. It was not only used to flavor foods, but it was indispensable in preserving them. In an age that had no freezers or refrigerators, salt kept food from spoiling. Salt solutions were used medically, specifically in washing newborn infants. Rock salt was also used as a fertilizer. Salt's value came from these many uses. Because of its value, Roman officers were given a salt allowance as part of their compensation. Our word *salary* is derived from that allowance, the *salarium*. When Jesus attested to the value of His disciples in the world, perhaps He had both salt's ability to flavor, as well as its ability to preserve in mind. Jesus' disciples are to flavor the world around them with God's love and direction; and they are to preserve that which is valuable in life from the spoilage caused by sin and hate. Christians who hold back from performing the function they are to have as salt are like salt that has lost its saltiness. In this passage, Jesus is probably alluding to rock salt, from which the salt could wash out. The resulting saltless white powder was used as a pavement for roads.

MATTHEW 5:14

light. Light is another basic element of life. The function of light is to illuminate the darkness. This is an image for the truth Christians are to bring to the world.
of the world. Israel was to be a light for the Gentiles (see Isa. 49:6). That function is now passed on to the followers of Jesus.

MATTHEW 5:15–16
light

The very purpose of light is defeated if it is hidden away. In the same way, Jesus' disciples are not to live secretly, but to live openly so that others can see who and what they are. The purpose of all this is not to focus on them, but to get people focused on God. Only if we give glory to God for what we do will this happen.

MATTHEW 5:16
say and do

let your light shine before men. What constitutes the "light" of Christians is what they say and do.
praise your Father. While persecution is the response that some people make toward those who embody the qualities of God's kingdom (Matt. 5:10), others will recognize in these qualities the character of God and give praise to Him.

notes:

Session

5

Spiritual Disciplines in My Life

Prepare for the Session

	READINGS	REFLECTIVE QUESTIONS
Monday	1 Corinthians 9:24	What is the "prize" you are hoping to win in life?
Tuesday	1 Corinthians 9:24	What obstacles have you encountered along the racetrack of life?
Wednesday	1 Corinthians 9:25	Evaluate your spiritual life in light of this verse.
Thursday	1 Corinthians 9:25	What do you want to hear God say to you at the end of your life?
Friday	1 Corinthians 9:26	What is God's purpose for your life?
Saturday	1 Corinthians 9:27	What spiritual disciplines are a part of your life?
Sunday	1 Corinthians 9:27	What spiritual disciplines do you need to develop?

notes:

OUR GOALS FOR
THIS SESSION ARE:

In groups of 6–8, gather people in a horseshoe configuration.

Make sure everyone has a name tag.

Take time to share information on class parties that are coming up as well as any relevant church events.

INTRODUCE THE ICEBREAKER ACTIVITY: The students have been given instructions in their books.

After the Icebreaker say something like, "Discipline and training tend to bring out the best in people. When people train in a disciplined way, they reach their optimum performance level. Today we will look at how spiritual disciplines bring out our spiritual best."

Hand out the Prayer/Praise Report. A sample copy is on pages 158-159. Have people write down prayer requests and praises. Then have the prayer coordinator collect the report and make copies for use during the Caring Time.

BIBLE STUDY
- to understand how disciplining ourselves spiritually is like how an athlete disciplines himself or herself
- to learn how to make spiritual discipline a part of our lives
- to talk about the importance of living a spiritually disciplined life

LIFE CHANGE
- to commit to a regular prayer time and a time set aside to be with God
- to set a goal for personal Bible reading
- to plan a spiritual life retreat

Icebreaker (10-15 minutes)

Bring Out Your Best. Go around the group on the first question. Then go around on the next question.

1. Finish this sentence: "If you want to bring out my best, then …"

   ☐ feed me!
   ☐ compliment my appearance
   ☐ put me around playful people
   ☐ give me a charge card and send me to the mall!
   ☐ give me a challenge
   ☐ give me lots of hugs
   ☐ put me in a competitive situation
   ☐ other: _____

2. Finish this sentence: "If you want to bring out my worst, then …"

   ☐ put me in a messy room
   ☐ try telling me what to do
   ☐ try putting me on a committee
   ☐ give me a charge card and send me to the mall!
   ☐ criticize me
   ☐ make me eat health food
   ☐ put me in a competitive situation
   ☐ other: _____

notes:

LEARNING FROM
THE BIBLE

**1 CORINTHIANS
9:24–27**

**Have one class
member, selected
ahead of time, read
the passage from
1 Corinthians.**

Bible Study (30-45 minutes)

The Scripture for this week:

²⁴*Do you not know that in a race all the runners run, but only one gets the prize? Run in such a way as to get the prize.* ²⁵*Everyone who competes in the games goes into strict training. They do it to get a crown that will not last; but we do it to get a crown that will last forever.* ²⁶*Therefore I do not run like a man running aimlessly; I do not fight like a man beating the air.* ²⁷*No, I beat my body and make it my slave so that after I have preached to others, I myself will not be disqualified for the prize.*

notes:

**Summarize these
introductory remarks.
Be sure to include
the underlined
information, which
gives the answers
to the student book
questions (provided
in the margin).**

...about today's session (5 minutes)

A DISCIPLINED LIFE

We are a culture that idolizes its athletes. We pay them exceedingly high salaries. They advertise every product imaginable, and our children wear articles of clothing with their names or numbers on them. We see the successes of these athletes on television, but most often we don't see the work it took to get them there. Only occasionally, in movies like *Rocky* or *Chariots of Fire*, do we see the hundreds of training hours of jumping rope or jogging through ocean surf. The year 2000 was an Olympic year, and one of the benefits of the extensive coverage of that event was hearing or reading about the training habits of the competitors. For instance, we read of swimmer <u>Lenny Krayzelburg</u> who emigrated with his family from the Soviet Union to the United States in 1989. The Krayzelburgs had very little money and no car, so when he first arrived in America at age 14, <u>Lenny had to commute to swim practice by foot or bus almost an hour each way</u>. He didn't get back home until 9:30 each night.[1] Or we read

*What examples of
discipline by athletes
are referred to in
this presentation?*

What other examples can you think of?

about <u>Marla Runyan, a runner who is legally blind</u> (20/300 vision in one eye and 20/400 vision in the other). <u>She had to learn to run hurdles by counting the steps between them.</u>[2] <u>Dave Scott</u>, a five-time iron man winner, exemplifies the vigor of an athlete's training program. <u>As an adult he worked 55 hours a week as a swimming instructor, swam 7000 yards a day, lifted weights for an hour or two, and ran 30–35 miles a week.</u> And that was *before* he got serious about training for triathlons.[3]

notes:

5

↻ Remain in groups of 6–8 people, in a horseshoe configuration.

In this small-group session, students will be responding to the following questions that will help them share their stories in terms of Paul's words about the race of life in 1 Corinthians 9:24–27.

Have the students explore these questions together.

Identifying with the Story (5-7 minutes)

1. What did you do as a teen that required practice or discipline?

   ☐ playing a sport
   ☐ being in a play or musical
   ☐ getting my homework done
   ☐ playing a musical instrument
   ☐ dancing or cheerleading
   ☐ other: _____

2. How well did you discipline yourself for the activity in question 1?

   ☐ I was a real slacker.
   ☐ A parent had to remind me.
   ☐ I did it—*most* of the time.
   ☐ I was my own drill sergeant.

3. Finish this sentence: "The goal in my life that I have been most disciplined in trying to reach has been ... ."

Share with your class the following information which you may modify according to your own perspectives and teaching needs. The answers to the student book questions (provided in the margin) are underlined.

Where else in Scripture did Paul use athletic imagery?

today's session (15-20 minutes)

Was the apostle Paul an athlete in his younger years? We will never know, but it appears that he was a fan of sports because he uses sports imagery on a number of occasions. Not only do we have the example of our text for this week, but in Philippians 3:14 he writes of pressing "on toward the goal to win the prize for which God has called me heavenward in Christ Jesus." In Galatians 5:7, he challenges the Galatians with the words, "You were running a good race. Who cut in on you and kept you from obeying the truth?" And in 2 Timothy 4:7 he summarizes his life with the words, "I have fought the good fight, I have finished the race." For a sports-crazy society like ours, it would seem that Paul knew how to speak our language! Let's see what he is saying to us in the sports imagery of 1 Corinthians 9.

Paul's comments in this section of the Bible can be put in two categories: (1) the nature of the prize that we pursue, and (2) the nature of the training necessary to get that prize.

The Nature of the Prize

Paul refers to how in a race only one person wins the prize. This is certainly emphasized in modern sports. "No one remembers who came in second," we are told by the zealous coaches of the world. For years before they first won the Super Bowl in 1997, the Denver Broncos were called "losers" because they had lost the Super Bowl so many times. Nobody spoke much of what an achievement it was to *go* so many times. But, this is not the way it is in the spiritual life! There is certainly not just one winner there. Aren't we told by Jesus in John 14:2, " 'In my Father's house are many rooms; if it were not so, I would have told you. I am going there to prepare a place for you' "? Perhaps the best way to understand Paul's words is to say that we should run the race of our spiritual lives with the same vigor *as if* there were only one winner and we wanted that person to be us. Certainly you can only take an analogy so far, but for a culture like ours where we are used to competition that inspires discipline and hard work, such an allusion makes sense. Although there is enough of the "prize" to go around, and more, we should still discipline ourselves as if there would be only one winner.

How should we apply Paul's reference to "only one gets the prize" to our spiritual lives?

The most essential thing Paul says about the "prize" is that this prize will last forever. Athletes compete for a transitory prize. That was especially true in ancient Greece, where the prize was a wreath that withered in a very short time. Olympic gold medals and Super Bowl rings last much longer, but even they are not forever. The adulation, fame, and money that are big parts of what drive athletes do not last

What athlete can you think of who was once revered but is now booed or forgotten by others?

much longer than a wreath. Last year's heroes are quickly old news, and if they aren't performing to their old standards *now*, they may even be booed by the crowds that once adored them.

In contrast, the prize for which Christians run their race is being part of God's eternal kingdom. As the song "Amazing Grace" says, "When we've been there ten thousand years, bright shining as the sun, we've no less days to sing God's praise than when we first begun." In addition to our own salvation, what we contribute to God's kingdom will never be forgotten by our God. If we win someone to Jesus Christ, that soul will shine eternally for all to see and the love we show to people by caring for their needs is an investment in the strengthening of an eternal soul.

The Nature of Our Training

Since our prize is an eternal one, that ought to motivate us all the more to take our Christian walk seriously, and discipline ourselves to live the Christian life with excellence. Hear the language the apostle Paul used to speak of how seriously he took *his* training: "I do not run like a man running aimlessly; I do not fight like a man beating the air. No, I beat my body and make it my slave so that after I have preached to others, I myself will not be disqualified for the prize" (v. 26). The language may seem extreme: "beat my body." But Paul has switched to a slavery image here. He was saying that either he had to get his body and physical impulses to be his slave, or he would be a slave to his body's impulses. We don't have to look far to find people who are enslaved by physical impulses. Their cravings tell them: "I need a cigarette! I need a cigarette!" There are seriously overweight people who cannot seem to stop overeating. Their cravings tell them: "More food! More food!" There are people who want a stable, faithful marriage relationship, but over and over again they surrender to the physical desires of the body. The issue becomes, "Who is going to be in charge and who is going to submit, me or my body?"

What does Paul mean when he speaks of beating his body?

Tools for Training

Spiritual discipline is what helps us to be in charge. And just like there are standard tools of training in the athlete's arsenal, like weight-training, jumping rope, stretching exercises, etc., so there are standard tools for our spiritual training. The first of these is *prayer*. Prayer calls on all of the resources of God to be at our disposal. Jesus said, " 'Ask and it will be given to you; seek and you will find; knock and the door will be opened to you' " (Matt. 7:7). But to be this kind of resource, prayer has to be more than what we do when we are in trouble and at our wit's end. It has to be something we do as a regular habit, like exercising. Doctors tell us that there is nothing worse for a person's heart than to go out and do vigorous exercise once in a

What tools of spiritual discipline are referred to in this presentation?

5

today's session (cont'd)

blue moon when the body isn't used to it. Conditioning comes from regular exercise, and that is true with prayer as well. We need to pray during the day as we confront our challenges, as well as in a regular prayer time, such as at night before bed or in the morning upon rising, when we can focus on God. Prayer needs to include taking time to listen to God as well as talking to God.

Our prayer time should also include time for *silence*. We live surrounded by noise. We talk of "noise pollution" and it's a good term. When do we take time to just be quiet? Psalm 46:10 tells us, "Be still, and know that I am God." Such quiet time not only helps us get in touch with God, but it also helps us get in touch with ourselves. *What am I really looking for in life? Where have I been? Where am I going? Where have I seen and experienced God along my path?* Getting away from other people (who can often dominate our thinking) can also help us get in touch with these issues. Many people use spiritual life retreats to do this. These can either be an individual retreat or a group retreat where people have individual quiet time.

We also need time for *devotional reading*. This should include Scripture reading and reading Christian books about issues we are facing. People who are part of a family should also include family devotional time and prayer, when they consider spiritual issues relevant to what family members face.

Worshiping with the family of God is an important discipline we share with other Christians. Hebrews 10:25 reminds us, "Let us not give up meeting together, as some are in the habit of doing, but let us encourage one another—and all the more as you see the Day approaching." This kind of corporate worship is not only essential to serving and praising God, it is also a source of encouragement as we face challenges in our Christian walk.

A discipline often overlooked by Protestants today is *fasting*. Fasting is a discipline which Christians have used through time to submit their physical impulses to God (Matt. 4:1–11). When a person is hungry and yet chooses not to eat, he or she is saying, "My physical impulses do not control me, God does." This discipline can also help us get in touch with the hunger and need of the world's starving people. However, this discipline must be used with care. We all know there are those who are bulimic or anorexic, and who use a refusal to eat as a way to destroy themselves. That is not what true fasting is about. While it is a private discipline, the watchcare of a spiritual director or mentor may be helpful (see Matt. 6:16–18).

Everyone likes to be part of a winning team. As Christians, we *are* part of such a team. But what we contribute to that team will depend in large part on how willing we are to discipline ourselves.

notes:

U **Remain in groups of 6–8 people, in a horseshoe configuration.**

In this small-group session, students will be applying the lessons of the text to their own lives through the following questions.

The students were asked (in the student book) to choose an answer for each question and explain why.

Learning from the Story (5-7 minutes)

1. If an athlete disciplined himself or herself the way you do in your spiritual life, would he or she most likely be:

   ☐ a superstar
   ☐ a consistent winner
   ☐ one generally found in the middle of the pack
   ☐ a lifelong second-stringer
   ☐ cut in training camp
   ☐ laughed off the team

2. In order to strengthen your spiritual life, which of the following spiritual disciplines do you *most* need to work on?

   ☐ regular worship with the family of God
   ☐ maintaining a disciplined prayer life
   ☐ regular Bible and devotional reading
   ☐ making time for silence and solitude
   ☐ special disciplines like fasting and taking spiritual life retreats
   ☐ other: _____

3. What help could you use from others in this group to do what you said you need to do in question 2?

   ☐ prayer
   ☐ suggestions on how to make time in my schedule for this discipline
   ☐ direction for Bible and devotional reading
   ☐ someone to check up on me and keep me honest—like my parent(s) used to!
   ☐ someone to pray with
   ☐ someone to go with me on a spiritual life retreat
   ☐ other: _____

5

life change lessons (5-7 minutes)

How can you remind yourself of planned quiet or devotional time?

Your choice of a Bible study goal would be:

We all know the difficulties that can be inherent in disciplining our-selves. Some of us have probably been *talking* a long time about starting to exercise or going on a diet or stopping smoking. It's another thing to start the process of discipline and self-denial. Look around you at the people in the class. We can all help and encourage each other in this matter. Let's resolve together to do just that in regard to our spiritual lives. Here are some steps we should all vow to take:

1. COMMIT TO A REGULAR PRAYER AND DEVOTIONAL TIME. If you have not already done so, this is essential. <u>Make sure you write it in your day planner or put it in your computer or cell phone reminder.</u> If you are part of a family, start by scheduling one family devotional time each week.

2. SET A GOAL FOR PERSONAL BIBLE READING. Start with the New Testament and decide how long you should take to read the whole thing. You might also go to a Christian bookstore and find some books that speak to your need or that help you with the Bible book you are reading in your devotional time. Keep such books in a visible place to remind you to read them.

3. PLAN A SPIRITUAL LIFE RETREAT. This should include time for solitude and silence. Your group may want to plan a joint retreat, or you might see if any are planned in your church or community.

♘ CARING TIME
Remain in groups of 6–8 people, in a horseshoe configuration.

Hand out the Prayer/ Praise Report to the entire group. Ask each subgroup to pray for the empty chair. Pray specifically for God to guide you to someone to bring next week to fill that chair.

Caring Time (15-20 minutes)

Remember that this time is for developing and expressing your caring for each other as group members by sharing any personal prayer requests and praying for each other's needs. Pray for the group member to your right that he or she will be able to follow through in the discipline he or she most wants to work on. Also, use the Prayer/Praise Report and pray for the concerns listed.

After a sufficient time of prayer in subgroups, close in a corporate prayer. Say, "Next week we will talk about: 'Caring for Others.' "

Remind participants of the daily Scripture readings and reflective questions found on page 58.

notes:

Reference Notes

Use these notes to gain further understanding
of the text as you study on your own.

**1 CORINTHIANS
9:24–27**
athletes

Paul turns to an athletic image to communicate the importance of self-discipline in the Christian life. This provides a transition to the call in chapter 10 to watch oneself and to forsake those things that would tempt one to fall away from Christ.

1 CORINTHIANS 9:24
the prize

only one gets the prize. Paul is not implying that in the spiritual life there is only one winner. All who put their faith in Christ and discipline themselves to do His will are winners. However, we should discipline ourselves *as if* there would be only one winner.

1 CORINTHIANS 9:25
the victory

crown. In the Greek games, the winner received a crown made of pine boughs. While simple and insignificant by today's standards, this crown conveyed a great deal of prestige. This prize was placed at the end of the race so that runners ran with their eyes on it. The Christian's prize is certainly more significant—eternal life with God. We must run our race, keeping our eyes on that prize.

1 CORINTHIANS 9:26
purpose

A runner in a race cannot simply run in any direction he or she chooses. The runner must stay on the course. Also, no boxer who swings wildly at the air will ever win, but rather those who concentrate on their opponent achieve victory.

1 CORINTHIANS 9:27
discipline

Paul applies the boxing imagery to himself as he wraps up his discussion of freedom in this chapter. Just as it is important for him to discipline his bodily urges (1 Cor. 6:12–17) so that he might be faithful to Christ's call, so, too, the Corinthians must exercise their Christian freedom in light of their responsibility to love. Otherwise, both he and they might be disqualified from God's race, like runners who left the track. Love, not "knowledge" (1 Cor. 8:1), is the essential demonstration of true faith.

5

notes:

[1] *AMI Specials Salutes Our Athletes: Olympics USA* (Boca Raton, FL: American Media Special, September, 2000), 51.

[2] Ibid., 25

[3] Dave Scott, *Dave Scott's Triathlon Training Manual* (New York: Simon & Schuster, 1986), 16.

Session

6

Caring for Others

Prepare for the Session

	READINGS	REFLECTIVE QUESTIONS
Monday	1 John 4:7–8	How are you doing at loving others?
Tuesday	1 John 4:9–10	Think about Christ's sacrifice for you—and fall in love with Him all over again.
Wednesday	1 John 4:11–12	How do you act toward your "dear friends"?
Thursday	1 John 4:13–16	How do you know that Christ lives in you?
Friday	1 John 4:17	Are you looking forward in confidence to meeting Christ on the Day of Judgment? Why or why not?
Saturday	1 John 4:18	What fears are you dealing with?
Sunday	1 John 4:19–21	Are there any Christian brothers or sisters you need to forgive—and love?

notes:

OUR GOALS FOR
THIS SESSION ARE:

In groups of 6–8, gather people in a horseshoe configuration.

Make sure everyone has a name tag.

Take time to share information on class parties that are coming up as well as any relevant church events.

INTRODUCE THE ICEBREAKER ACTIVITY: The students have been given instructions in their books.

After the Icebreaker say something like, "Have you heard the saying, 'There are no strangers—only friends we have not met'? That is how we are called to look upon each other in Jesus Christ. In today's session, we will consider what it means to be called to care for each other as friends in Christ."

Hand out the Prayer/Praise Report. A sample copy is on pages 158–159. Have people write down prayer requests and praises. Then have the prayer coordinator collect the report and make copies for use during the Caring Time.

BIBLE STUDY
- to consider what it means to love one another as the Bible calls us to
- to understand that Jesus is the perfect example of how we are to love each other
- to think through the importance to our witness of caring for others

LIFE CHANGE
- to make a caring initiative this week toward someone we have had trouble with in the past
- to set aside at least one hour a week to give to people in need
- to find one way to act more lovingly to our families

Icebreaker (10-15 minutes)

Old Friends. Friends are what make life good. They are also the ones who help you make it through when life is hard. Think back on some of your friendships.

1. Who did you consider your best friend (other than your spouse) during each of the following periods:

    ◇ childhood: _____
    ◇ adolescence: _____
    ◇ young adulthood: _____
    ◇ now: _____

2. Pick one of these friends and describe him or her to the group. How did he or she come through for you at a time when life was hard?

6

notes:

Bible Study   (30-45 minutes)

The Scripture for this week:

⁷Dear friends, let us love one another, for love comes from God. Everyone who loves has been born of God and knows God. ⁸Whoever does not love does not know God, because God is love. ⁹This is how God showed his love among us: He sent his one and only Son into the world that we might live through him. ¹⁰This is love: not that we loved God, but that he loved us and sent his Son as an atoning sacrifice for our sins. ¹¹Dear friends, since God so loved us, we also ought to love one another. ¹²No one has ever seen God; but if we love one another, God lives in us and his love is made complete in us.

¹³We know that we live in him and he in us, because he has given us of his Spirit. ¹⁴And we have seen and testify that the Father has sent his Son to be the Savior of the world. ¹⁵If anyone acknowledges that Jesus is the Son of God, God lives in him and he in God. ¹⁶And so we know and rely on the love God has for us.

God is love. Whoever lives in love lives in God, and God in him. ¹⁷In this way, love is made complete among us so that we will have confidence on the day of judgment, because in this world we are like him. ¹⁸There is no fear in love. But perfect love drives out fear, because fear has to do with punishment. The one who fears is not made perfect in love.

¹⁹We love because he first loved us. ²⁰If anyone says, "I love God," yet hates his brother, he is a liar. For anyone who does not love his brother, whom he has seen, cannot love God, whom he has not seen. ²¹And he has given us this command: Whoever loves God must also love his brother.

notes:

...about today's session (5 minutes)

WHAT IT MEANS TO LOVE

Summarize these introductory remarks. Be sure to include the underlined information, which gives the answers to the student book questions (provided in the margin).

In Nathaniel Hawthorne's classic American novel, *The Scarlet Letter*, there is an interesting contrast between the characters. Hester Prynne is a woman who has committed adultery, for which she is sentenced to wear a scarlet "A" for "adulterer" on the front of her clothing. A man, Roger Chillingworth, works throughout the story to get vengeance against her. He is the picture of the religious man, and one might expect that the sympathies of the readers might gravitate toward him as the standard-bearer for a moral life. However, that is not the case. In accordance with his last name, there is a coldness about Chillingworth's drive for vengeance that turns readers against him and toward the warmer, more human sinner, Hester Prynne. People seem to have a natural revulsion for those who say they love God but are somehow cold toward other people. Interestingly enough, our Scripture for today says God has essentially the same attitude. God may also prefer the Hester Prynnes of the world to the Roger Chillingworths.

What does the leader say that people have a natural revulsion for?

What does this say to us as we seek to be Christian witnesses? Certainly it does not mean that we need to condone sin in order to be liked. What it does mean, however, is that we need to keep love of people as an aim that is higher than anything else save love of God Himself. We cannot love people and revel in their moral downfalls. We cannot love people and sit high above them like Jonah, waiting for God to "zap" them (see Jonah 4:1–11). We cannot love God and do anything less than rejoice when someone receives God's forgiveness, even for sins committed against us. To love people is to love the grace of God that saves them.

6

According to this presentation, "To love people is to love _____."

In this session we will look at what it means to genuinely care for people. We will look at the inherent contradiction between saying we love God but being cold toward someone else also struggling with sin. And we will consider what it means to model our love of others after the greatest lover of all—God.

notes:

Remain in groups of 6–8 people, in a horseshoe configuration.

In this small-group session, students will be responding to the following questions that will help them share their stories in terms of John's teaching about love in 1 John 4:7–21.

Have the students explore these questions together.

Identifying with the Story (5-7 minutes)

1. When you were a child, who defined love for you by the way he or she treated you and others? What one act can you remember that particularly illustrates this person's loving nature?

2. What has God done for you that has helped drive home the truth that "God is love"?

3. Which of the following phrases from this biblical text is most meaningful to you at this point in your life?

   ☐ "Whoever does not love does not know God, because God is love" (v. 8)—I'm tired of pious people who really don't care about me.

   ☐ "This is love: not that we loved God, but that he loved us and sent his Son" (v. 10)—This is the essence of the gospel.

   ☐ "No one has ever seen God; but if we love one another, God lives in us" (v. 12)—I got to know God through people who showed me His love.

   ☐ "There is no fear in love. But perfect love drives out fear" (v. 18)—God's love is more powerful than anything I fear!

   ☐ Other: _____

notes:

today's session (15-20 minutes)

Share with your class the following information which you may modify according to your own perspectives and teaching needs. The answers to the student book questions (provided in the margin) are underlined.

What is the difference in the meaning of the Greek words eros and agape?

A form of the word *love* is used at least 25 times in the 15 verses of this text, depending somewhat on the version you read. That certainly establishes it as an important theme in what John is telling his readers! His message is echoed in a 1960s Dusty Springfield song that said the world needs love. But John's concept of what love is and how it needs to be expressed is far different than many people in the world. In the '60s, people proclaimed, "Make love, not war," but what they meant was <u>the sexual love that the Greeks called *eros*</u>. While good in its place, erotic love does not necessarily bring healing to the world. Used promiscuously it brings us diseases like AIDS, social problems like teen mothers trying to raise children while working at minimum-wage jobs, and the emotional and relational conflicts that are fodder for our soap operas and supermarket tabloids.

A Biblical View of Love

When John spoke of love, he was speaking of something much different. <u>He was referring to what the Greeks called *agape*. This is love that gives without expecting return.</u> This is <u>love that shows concern for another's ultimate well-being.</u> This is <u>love that emulates God's love.</u> Let's look at our Scripture for this week and discover more specifically what this love is like.

6

First of all, we learn that this kind of love for others goes hand-in-hand with loving God. "Whoever does not love does not know God, because God is love" (v. 8). Furthermore, "If anyone says, 'I love God,' yet hates his brother, he is a liar. For anyone who does not love his brother, whom he has seen, cannot love God, whom he has not seen" (v. 20). This is a consistent emphasis of the Bible. Jesus tells us in <u>Matthew 25:31–46</u> that when we do acts of love for the people around us, like clothing the naked, feeding the hungry, and visiting the sick and imprisoned, it is like we are doing it for Him. Even as far back as the Old Testament prophets, God said that He didn't want people coming to "worship" Him while living a life of violence and injustice toward the people around them (see <u>Isa. 1:10–20; Mic. 6:6–8; Amos 5:21–24</u>).

What other Scriptures indicate a connection between loving God and loving people?

Learning from God How to Love

What are three things we can learn from how God loves us in Jesus Christ and how we are to love other people?

Another important thing we learn is that if we want to know the true nature of love, we should study how God loved us when He sent His Son, Jesus Christ. "This is love: not that we loved God, but that he loved us and sent his Son as an atoning sacrifice for our sins" (v. 10). We need to look at what God did when He sent Jesus, and we can do this by looking at some other Scriptures. <u>One thing we learn is that God cared enough to *initiate the love relationship*</u>. We did

today's session (cont'd)

not have such a love for who created us that we went out looking for a way to love Him. Rather, He cared enough about us to be the initiator and show His love for us. The apostle Paul tells us in Romans 5:8, "God demonstrates his own love for us in this: While we were still sinners, Christ died for us." God didn't wait for us to start straightening out our lives and reach out to Him. He was the initiator. In Isaiah 65:1, God says through Isaiah, " 'I revealed myself to those who did not ask for me; I was found by those who did not seek me. To a nation that did not call on my name, I said, "Here am I, here am I." ' " Being the initiator involves a lot more risk because the one you are reaching out to can reject you. That is the risk God took with us. And that is the kind of love that God calls for in us. It's harder to love that neighbor who drives right past without noticing you, or that coworker who treats you like a cog in the business machinery. But doing so is what God's love is about.

Name two other Bible passages that tell of how God showed the initiative in loving us.

A second thing we learn about love from what God did is that love is *action-oriented*. Love is not just nice, "warm fuzzy" feelings. It's action. Because God loved, He sent His Son. James tells us how essential such action is to truly show love: "What good is it, my brothers, if a man claims to have faith but has no deeds? Can such faith save him? Suppose a brother or sister is without clothes and daily food. If one of you says to him, 'Go, I wish you well; keep warm and well fed,' but does nothing about his physical needs, what good is it?" (Jas. 2:14–16). Jesus also told a parable to emphasize the importance of action over words. He told the story of a father who told his two sons to go work in the vineyard. The first said he would not go, but in the end he decided to go. The second said he would go, but didn't follow through with action. Jesus said it was the first son who did what God wanted (Matt. 21:28–32). And so it is that saying good, loving things is not enough: we need to act.

What price did God pay to show His love for us?

A third thing we learn about love from God's love is that *love pays the price*. John tells us that not only did God send Jesus, but that Jesus became the "atoning sacrifice" for our sins (v. 10). For a loving relationship between us and our Holy God to be possible, something had to be done about the sin that separated us from Him. Sin demands the price of death (Rom. 6:23), and God was willing to pay that price through His only Son.

Paying the Price

What price are you willing to pay to love people? Will you leave the comfort and security of your home at night to go out and visit those who are sick, or those who are new to your town? Will you risk rejection by speaking up to defend those who are victims of racist jokes or stereotypes? Will you pay the price of being patient with people when they are going through a hard time, or are irritable and not very easy to love? It's easy to say nice things. It's much harder to pay such prices to truly love people. God did it to show what genuine love is. Will we follow God's example?

What the world needs now is genuine love, not sweet, syrupy sentiment or unbridled physical passion. What it needs is the *agape* of God—self-giving love that takes the initiative in reaching out to people and is willing to reach beyond words to act and pay the price. Are we willing to be part of bringing such love to our world?

notes:

6

Remain in groups of 6–8 people, in a horseshoe configuration.

In this small-group session, students will be applying the lessons of the text to their own lives through the following questions.

The students were asked (in the student book) to choose an answer for each question and explain why.

Learning from the Story (5-7 minutes)

1. What qualities make it harder for you to love people as a "brother or sister whom you have seen"? How does this passage challenge you in relationship to such people?

2. What do you learn from how God expresses His love toward you, in relation to how He expects you to love other people?

3. If you were to take this passage seriously, what would be the first thing you would have to change about the way you relate to others?

Share with the class the following thoughts on how the lessons of this text might be applied today. The answers to the student book questions (provided in the margin) are underlined unless the question requires a personal answer.

To what does James compare those who hear the Word of God but don't act on it?

Three concrete ways you could put caring for others into action are:

life change lessons (5-7 minutes)

James reminds us, "Do not merely listen to the word, and so deceive yourselves. Do what it says. <u>Anyone who listens to the word but does not do what it says is like a man who looks at his face in a mirror and, after looking at himself, goes away and immediately forgets what he looks like</u>" (Jas. 1:22–24). We have just looked at ourselves in the mirror of Scripture. Most of us have probably seen some things that are not very "presentable" about ourselves in the way we treat others. Are we just going to walk away and forget about it, or are we going to fix what is wrong, as we would if we looked in an actual mirror and saw a splotch of mustard on our nose? Here are some things we ought to consider doing:

1. <u>MAKE A CARING INITIATIVE TOWARD SOMEONE YOU HAVE HAD TROUBLE WITH IN THE PAST</u>. Remember how God took the initiative toward us in Jesus Christ? That is what we also ought to do. This could be anything from just giving them a call and asking them how things are going to volunteering to help them with a project.

2. <u>SET ASIDE AT LEAST ONE HOUR A WEEK TO GIVE TO PEOPLE IN NEED</u>. This could mean visiting the sick or elderly, helping with a food program, raising funds for a charity, or helping with a youth ministry.

3. <u>FIND ONE WAY TO ACT MORE LOVINGLY TO YOUR FAMILY</u>. It's not a good witness to reach out to strangers while neglecting those under your own roof! This might mean quietly doing that chore everyone argues about (such as taking out the trash!), or setting aside time each day to play with your children or talk with your spouse, or (if you live alone) making sure you call your parent(s) or grandparent(s) on a regular basis.

notes:

PRAYER OF COMMITMENT

"Lord Jesus, I need you. I realize I'm a sinner, and I can't save myself. I need Your mercy. I believe that You are the Son of God, that You died on the cross for my sins and rose from the dead. I repent of my sins and put my faith in You as Savior and Lord. Take control of my life, and help me follow You in obedience. In Jesus' name. Amen."

 Caring Time (15-20 minutes)

Close by praying for one another. Pray for God's love to fill you in a new way and to help you take the "first step" you talked about in question 3 of "Learning from the Story." In addition, pray for the concerns on the Prayer/Praise Report.

Conclude your prayer time by reading together the words of Jesus in John 17:20–23:

My prayer is not for them alone. I pray also for those who will believe in me through their message, that all of them may be one, Father, just as you are in me and I am in you. May they also be in us so that the world may believe that you have sent me. I have given them the glory that you gave me, that they may be one as we are one: I in them and you in me. May they be brought to complete unity to let the world know that you sent me and have loved them even as you have loved me.

6

notes:

Note: If there are people in your group who have not accepted Christ as Savior, you may want to lead your group in praying this prayer.

Then, ask folks to talk with you privately to discuss the next steps.

CARING TIME
Remain in groups of 6–8 people, in a horseshoe configuration.

Hand out the Prayer/Praise Report to the entire group. Ask each subgroup to pray for the empty chair. Pray specifically for God to guide you to someone to bring next week to fill that chair.

After a sufficient time of prayer in subgroups, close in a corporate prayer. Say, "Next week we will talk about: 'Learning to Affirm.' "

Remind participants of the daily Scripture readings and reflective questions found on page 70.

✝

BIBLE STUDY NOTES

1 JOHN 4:7
love each other

1 JOHN 4:8
God's nature

1 JOHN 4:10
atoning sacrifice

1 JOHN 4:11
love demonstrated

1 JOHN 4:12
love seen

1 JOHN 4:13–16

1 JOHN 4:18
no fear

Reference Notes

Use these notes to gain further understanding
of the text as you study on your own.

love one another. John uses this phrase three times in five verses (see vv. 7,11,12). Each time, however, he uses it in a slightly different way. Here he urges his readers to love others because love originates in God. *Everyone who loves.* Since "love comes from God," all acts of love are reflections of God's nature in the believer.

God is love. This is the second great assertion that John makes in this epistle about the nature of God. (His first assertion is that God is light.) This is one of the first truths we teach our children in Sunday school, and this is appropriate. To say that God is love is to say that love is at the core of God's nature, and so as children begin to know Him, this is a good place to start.

Love is initiated by God. It is given substance by the incarnation of His Son. *an atoning sacrifice for our sins.* By this phrase John describes the saving work that Jesus did on behalf of the human race, thus opening up the way back to fellowship with God. The concept of atonement is seen in the Old Testament practice of substitution and sacrifice. In the Old Testament, sin was dealt with when a person symbolically placed his or her sins on an animal that was brought to the temple. This animal had to be perfect—without spot or blemish. It was then sacrificed in place of the sinful (imperfect) person. Such substitutionary sacrifices were a picture of what Jesus would one day do for all people on the cross.

love one another. The second use of this phrase. The basis for this exhortation is the demonstrated fact that "God so loved us." Jesus' sacrificial death as atonement for sin on behalf of the human race shows people the depth of God's love and should thus release in them the ability to love others. Because they are loved, they can love.

love one another. In the third use of this phrase, John states that although God cannot be seen directly, His love can be experienced as Christians love others. Since God is love, they know Him when they love.

The Holy Spirit testifies to us that Jesus is God's Son. That's how we can know that when Jesus showed love, He was showing us something about the nature of God Himself.

no fear in love. The reason for the confidence believers will have on the Day of Judgment is that they know God to be their loving Father (in whose love they have dwelt). To know you are loved by someone is to trust that he or she will never harm you and that you have nothing to fear in their presence. To know that God loves us is to know that we have nothing to fear because we know that God is more powerful than anything else in the universe. God's love trumps all of our enemies.

1 JOHN 4:18 (cont'd)

✝ *fear has to do with punishment.* This is the heart of the relationship of people who approach God in fear: they think God is going to punish them. But if we are in Christ, then we need not fear punishment; rather, we rest assured of God's loving forgiveness.

1 JOHN 4:19

The love believers exhibit is a response to the prior love of God for them. Love begets love.

1 JOHN 4:20
a contradiction

Love for God is not merely warm, fuzzy feelings. Love is not love unless it finds concrete expression via active caring for others. Furthermore, since it is far easier to love a visible person than to love the invisible God, to claim success in the harder task while failing in the easier task is an absurd and hopeless contradiction.

1 JOHN 4:21
the command

If people truly love God they will keep His commands, and His command is to love others. John reminds his readers of this one more time as he ends this session on love (see also 2:9–11; 3:10,23). To love God and to love others is a single, inseparable command.

notes:

6

69

Session

7

Learning to Affirm

Prepare for the Session

	READINGS	REFLECTIVE QUESTIONS
Monday	1 Thessalonians 1:2	Who do you thank God for consistently?
Tuesday	1 Thessalonians 1:3	What does your faith, love, and hope produce?
Wednesday	1 Thessalonians 1:4	Think about what it means to be chosen by God.
Thursday	1 Thessalonians 1:5	What sacrifices have you made for the sake of your witness among your friends and neighbors?
Friday	1 Thessalonians 1:6	Does knowing Christ as Savior fill your heart with joy? Why or why not?
Saturday	1 Thessalonians 1:7	How can you model Christ to other believers?
Sunday	1 Thessalonians 1:8–10	Is your faith known "everywhere"? Where is it known the most?

notes:

BIBLE STUDY

- to take note of the consistency with which the apostle Paul affirmed the people in the churches to which he wrote
- to consider the effect of affirming other people on their work and witness
- to understand how a Christian community that practices affirmation can develop a stronger oneness with each other

LIFE CHANGE

- to write letters or emails of thanks to three different people within the next week
- to tell two different people at work what we appreciate about their work
- to affirm each suggestion that is made in the next meeting we attend

Icebreaker   (10-15 minutes)

Bullish On People. Over the past few weeks, we have "invested" in each other as a group. What kinds of investments have group members turned out to be? Look at the list and find a person in this group who best fits each category. Share these with each other in a spirit of affirmation.

BLUE CHIP STOCK: reliable one, performing steady and true

GROWTH STOCK: the one who has grown and "shot up" the most during these sessions

PASSBOOK SAVINGS: not flashy, but always available to the group

PRECIOUS METALS: showing his or her inherent (self) worth

COMMODITY FUTURES: one who shows a lot of potential for growth beyond this group

MUTUAL FUND: one with diverse strengths that contributed to the group

REAL ESTATE: where we invested a lot, but got a lot in return

RARE ART: one whose beauty as a person made it a pleasure to invest

7

notes:

LEARNING FROM THE BIBLE

1 THESSALONIANS 1:2–10

Have a member of the class, selected ahead of time, read the passage from 1 Thessalonians.

Bible Study (30-45 minutes)

The Scripture for this week:

²*We always thank God for all of you, mentioning you in our prayers.* ³*We continually remember before our God and Father your work produced by faith, your labor prompted by love, and your endurance inspired by hope in our Lord Jesus Christ.*

⁴*For we know, brothers loved by God, that he has chosen you,* ⁵*because our gospel came to you not simply with words, but also with power, with the Holy Spirit and with deep conviction. You know how we lived among you for your sake.* ⁶*You became imitators of us and of the Lord; in spite of severe suffering, you welcomed the message with the joy given by the Holy Spirit.* ⁷*And so you became a model to all the believers in Macedonia and Achaia.* ⁸*The Lord's message rang out from you not only in Macedonia and Achaia—your faith in God has become known everywhere. Therefore we do not need to say anything about it,* ⁹*for they themselves report what kind of reception you gave us. They tell how you turned to God from idols to serve the living and true God,* ¹⁰*and to wait for his Son from heaven, whom he raised from the dead—Jesus, who rescues us from the coming wrath.*

notes:

Summarize these introductory remarks. Be sure to include the underlined information, which gives the answers to the student book questions (provided in the margin).

What negative messages about yourself (like the one by Jonathan Edwards) do you remember hearing from pastors or church teachers in your spiritual journey? How did they affect you?

...about today's session (5 minutes)

AFFIRMING OTHERS

For centuries, Christianity was anything but affirming of people. Famed preacher and evangelist Jonathan Edwards, in his sermon "Sinners in the Hands of an Angry God," taught that people were "vile insects" that God hung by a thread over a flame. Many people who grew up in the church were taught that to say anything good about themselves was egotistical and saying anything good about someone else might give that person "a swelled head."

Do you agree that
"people work best
when they feel good
about themselves"?
Why or why not?

These attitudes, however, are not biblical. In every letter Paul writes, with the exception of Galatians (where he was very angry with those he thought were straying away from the gospel and toward legalism), he starts the letter by affirming the people of the church to which he is writing (see also Rom. 1:8; 1 Cor. 1:4; Eph. 1:15–16; Phil. 1:3; Col. 1:3; 2 Thess. 1:3). Paul seemed to realize that people work best when they feel good about themselves and what they have accomplished. That still holds true. We need to reclaim Paul's ministry of affirmation. In this session we will look at what that means.

notes:

Remain in groups of 6–8 people, in a horseshoe configuration.

In this small-group session, students will be responding to the following questions that will help them share their stories in terms of Paul's affirmation of the Thessalonians in 1 Thessalonians 1:2–10.

Have the students explore these questions together.

Identifying with the Story (5-7 minutes)

1. Paul describes how the gospel, the good news about Jesus, came to the people of the church at Thessalonica. Which of the following sets of words or phrases best describes how the good news came to you?

gradually   in a flash of insight
. . . .
with a quiet peace   with tears
. . . .
at a time of great   during a time of great
blessing in my life   conflict in my life

2. The Thessalonians imitated the Christian example of Paul and his coworkers. In your Christian growth, who have you sought to imitate?

3. Who in your life has most affirmed you, as Paul here affirms the Thessalonians?

7

Share with your class the following information which you may modify according to your own perspectives and teaching needs. The answers to the student book questions (provided in the margin) are underlined.

What spiritual leaders are mentioned as having used a positive and affirming approach to motivating people?

What did Jesus call Simon that affirmed him? What effect did this have on Simon?

Name two things Paul affirmed in the Thessalonians.

today's session (15-20 minutes)

How do you bring out the best in people? Some people seem to try it by reprimanding them or threatening them with punishment or failure. But the greatest leaders of our civilization have most often taken a more positive approach. For instance, Gandhi inspired millions of people to do great things. Louis Fischer, one of Gandhi's most important biographers, described the key to Gandhi's success in working with people as, "He refused to see the bad in people. He often changed human beings by regarding them not as what they were but as though they were what they wished to be, and as though the good in them was all of them."[1] But Gandhi was certainly not the first leader to use this approach. Jesus once took a man who had failed Him on a number of occasions and decided to call him *petra* or "rock." It was not a name you would expect to be given to a man with an erratic history, but Jesus affirmed Simon Peter because He knew the potential in him. Jesus' affirmation of Peter strengthened him and, in turn, strengthened the church.

Paul's Use of Affirmation

Paul also was a great affirmer of people. Let's look at how he expressed affirmation to the Thessalonians, and how such affirmation can strengthen a church's witness.

Paul starts by telling the Thessalonians he *thanks* God for them (v. 2). How appropriate that is! When you think about it, what do we have to thank God for more than the people God has given us and through whom He shows us love? We often tell people that we will pray for them, but do we also tell them that we thank God for them? To tell people that you thank God for them is to tell them just how precious they are to you.

Paul goes on to affirm *how the Thessalonians responded to the gospel*. Specifically, he says that "our gospel came to you not simply with words, but also with power, with the Holy Spirit and with deep conviction" (v. 5). At first glance, it might seem that Paul was affirming himself with that statement. But Paul knew that a receptive heart in those who were hearing the message was essential to a mission's success. When Jesus went to His hometown, He did not do many miracles there because of their lack of faith (see Matt. 13:53–58). That the gospel came to the Thessalonians "with power" is a testimony to how receptive their hearts were.

Paul reserved most of his words of praise for the way the Thessalonians *lived as a model of faith* after coming to Christ. Paul affirmed them for their "work produced by faith, ... labor prompted by love, and ... endurance inspired by hope in our Lord Jesus Christ"

(v. 3). Because of such qualities they became an exemplary church: "So you became a model to all the believers in Macedonia and Achaia. The Lord's message rang out from you not only in Macedonia and Achaia—your faith in God has become known everywhere" (vv. 7–8). Paul further says that he was not the only one who had taken note of their witness (vv. 9–10).

The Effect of Affirmation

What effect does such praise have on the ministry and witness of a church? Some might fear that it could make a church rest on its laurels, but the facts indicate the opposite. We have already seen how Paul used affirmation and that Paul's churches thrived is why most of the New Testament is concerned with either a description of Paul's work (most of Acts) or letters to his churches. But the principle holds true today as well. George Barna, founder of a Christian marketing research company, has studied what he calls "turn-around churches"—churches that had been going downhill in ministry and attendance but turned things around and thrived. He found a variety of factors that helped these churches turn around. One principle that he drew from this study was, "When people perform true ministry, they should be applauded." More specifically, he writes, "A successful ministry is one in which people are recognized for their accomplishments, not to place someone on a pedestal, but because human beings need to be recognized for their good works. ... Put in proper perspective, a bit of celebration and appreciation regarding true ministry can help maintain an active and happy congregation."[2]

What did George Barna find out about affirmation in "turn-around churches"?

Certainly what Barna says about turn-around churches is also what experts have found in other areas of life. In child-rearing, child psychologists have long said that parents can accomplish more by affirming what their children do right than they can by jumping all over them for what they do wrong. Foster Cline and Jim Fay write in *Parenting With Love and Logic*, "Unfortunately, many parents don't give their children a chance to build a positive self-concept—they concentrate on their children's weaknesses. ... But parents who build on their kids' strengths find their children growing in responsibility almost daily."[3] Whether it's parents and children or employers and employees, we benefit from applying Paul's treatment of his spiritual children.

Affirmation and Our Own Experience

When we stop to think about it, we can corroborate these findings by our own experiences and feelings. Which kind of church would *you* rather be part of—one where all you hear is bickering about what people are doing wrong, or one where every success, no matter how small, is affirmed and celebrated?

today's session (cont'd)

When people don't affirm each others' successes, but only criticize each other's failures, people tend to get discouraged. Why try? Nothing you do is ever good enough. Nothing you do ever gets rewarded. Affirmation helps us know that what we do well is appreciated by others and that motivates us to do well again.

What two things does affirming others in the context of the church do?

Learning to affirm others in the context of the church does two things: (1) <u>It helps people feel better about themselves, and (2) it strengthens the church</u>. It's natural that these two go together. When you help people feel good about themselves, it makes for a more joyful church, and a joyful church is a stronger church. When you strengthen the church, its message of God's love and forgiveness will be proclaimed with greater power. And that, in turn, helps people feel good about themselves! When you put together a joyous people and a strong church, the result is glory to the God who is Lord of both! That is the ultimate importance of learning to affirm one another.

notes:

✠

Learning from the Story (5-7 minutes)

☺ **Remain in groups of 6–8 people, in a horseshoe configuration.**

In this small-group session, students will be applying the lessons of the text to their own lives through the following questions.

The students were asked (in the student book) to choose an answer for each question and explain why.

1. Who do you know who has recently become a Christian whom you could affirm for the enthusiasm he or she shows for the gospel?

2. Who do you know who, like the Thessalonians, serves as a model to other believers? Have you affirmed this person for his or her witness?

3. In terms of the ease with which you affirm other people, how would you rate yourself on the following scale?

   . . . .

   I'm a perfectionist—
   my role is to tell people
   what they could do better!

   I'm an affirmer—
   my role is to "catch
   people doing right!"

life change lessons (5-7 minutes)

Share with the class the following thoughts on how the lessons of this text might be applied today. The answers to the student book questions (provided in the margin) are underlined unless the question requires a personal answer.

We have a tendency to act like _____, or how people acted _____.

What attitude do you need to have toward yourself when you slip back into a more negative approach?

While we might agree that it's best to affirm people rather than criticize them, changing what we actually do and say might be much harder. We have a tendency to act like <u>we have always acted</u>, or how people acted <u>in the family in which we were raised</u>. So we need to change these behaviors by disciplining ourselves with small steps over a period of time. If affirming others has not been our habit in the past, there will be times that we slip up, and go back to a more negative approach. <u>But we need to be patient and give ourselves the same affirmation we are giving to others</u>. That is, we need to affirm ourselves for the times we successfully gave affirmation instead of getting down on ourselves for those times we slipped up and were critical! Here are some concrete things we can do to begin this change:

1. WRITE LETTERS OR EMAILS OF THANKS TO THREE DIFFERENT PEOPLE WITHIN THE NEXT WEEK. These might be family, friends, or church members. Tell them why you thank God for them. Just write a few paragraphs to each so the writing task won't seem intimidating.

2. TELL TWO DIFFERENT PEOPLE AT WORK WHAT YOU APPRECIATE ABOUT THEIR WORK. Make sure what you say is sincere. See how it affects the way they relate to you. If you don't work outside the home, tell someone you do volunteer work with.

3. AFFIRM EACH SUGGESTION THAT IS MADE IN THE NEXT MEETING YOU ATTEND. This does not mean that you have to ultimately go along with every suggestion. It just means that you will look for and point out what is good about each suggestion.

7

notes:

Caring Time (15-20 minutes)

CARING TIME
Remain in groups of 6–8 people, in a horseshoe configuration.

Hand out the Prayer/Praise Report to the entire group. Ask each subgroup to pray for the empty chair. Pray specifically for God to guide you to someone to bring next week to fill that chair.

After a sufficient time of prayer in subgroups, close in a corporate prayer. Say, "Next week we will talk about: 'Being an Encourager.'"

Remind participants of the daily Scripture readings and reflective questions found on page 80.

Take time now to care for one another through prayer. Go around the group and have each person pray for the person on his or her right. Thank God for that person and for the good things you have seen in his or her life. Also, use the Prayer/Praise Report and pray for the concerns listed. Start with this sentence:

"Dear God, I thank you for my friend _____."

Close by asking God to give each group member the strength and wisdom to accomplish the life change goals from this session.

notes:

BIBLE STUDY NOTES

1 THESSALONIANS 1:2
affirmation

1 THESSALONIANS 1:3
essentials of faith

Reference Notes

Use these notes to gain further understanding of the text as you study on your own.

We always thank God for all of you. Paul usually began his letters with an affirmation of the recipients (see also Rom. 1:8; 1 Cor. 1:4; Eph. 1:15–16; Phil. 1:3; Col. 1:3; 2 Thess. 1:3).

faith ... love ... hope. Paul and other New Testament writers use these words (or a combination of two of them) as a way to sum up the essentials of the Christian life (see Rom. 5:1–5; 1 Cor. 13:13; Gal. 5:5–6; Eph. 4:2–5; Col. 1:4–5; 1 Thess. 5:8; Heb. 6:10–12; 10:22–24; 1 Peter 1:21–22). Faith in Christ, rooted in the hope of eternal life, is expressed by love to others. These are active concepts, the presence of which is seen by tangible activities of sacrifice and service. It is not that these activities earn God's favor, but that their presence is proof of having received God's favor (see also 1 Thess. 3:6; 4:9; 5:8).

✝

1 THESSALONIANS 1:4
one family

brothers loved by God. To pagans used to remote and unpredictable gods, this is a reminder of the intimacy with which God the Father relates to His people. Sharing in this common love is what makes the Gentile Thessalonians and the Jewish Paul brothers and sisters in God's family.
he has chosen you. Paul's purpose in reminding them of God's initiative in their salvation is to strengthen their hope in light of the pressures of external persecution (2:14) and internal uncertainty (4:13).

1 THESSALONIANS 1:5
power and conviction

our gospel came to you ... with power, with the Holy Spirit and with deep conviction. See Acts 17:1–9. The success of Paul's mission is seen in his commendation of the Thessalonians (vv. 2–3; 4:1,9) and by the reaction of his opponents who resorted to mob violence to stop his work (Acts 17:5).

1 THESSALONIANS 1:6
imitators

You became imitators of us and of the Lord. Discipleship means to become like one's teacher. Paul called people to imitate Christ (Eph. 5:1–2) and himself as a follower of Christ (1 Cor. 4:16; 11:1; Gal. 4:12; Phil. 3:17). In doing so, he echoed Jesus' call to " 'follow me' " (Mark 1:17; 8:34). The specific action commended here is their obedience to the gospel in spite of the opposition it created.

1 THESSALONIANS 1:7

Macedonia and Achaia. These are the northern and southern provinces that made up Greece. Thessalonica was in Macedonia.

1 THESSALONIANS 1:8
a clear witness

The Lord's message rang out from you. The story of their response to the gospel in the midst of conflict had spread throughout the area. Their location on a major Roman trade route and the intensity of the reaction to the gospel in their city easily accounts for the wide dispersion of their story.

7

1 THESSALONIANS 1:9
repentance

turned to God from idols. This illustrates repentance, a decisive rejection of one's past lifestyle and false beliefs to embrace a new way (see Acts 3:19; 9:35; 11:21; 2 Cor. 3:16).

1 THESSALONIANS 1:10
return of Christ

to wait for his Son from heaven. Uncertainty about the meaning and timing of the return of Christ led to the confusion this letter addresses.
the coming wrath. Both Jews and Christians foresaw a time when God would judge the earth. The gospel is the announcement that through faith in Christ believers are rescued from that judgment (John 3:36).

notes:

[1] Quoted in Alan Loy McGinnis, *The Friendship Factor* (Minneapolis, MN: Augsburg Press, 1979), 100.

[2] George Barna, *Turn-Around Churches* (Ventura, CA: Regal Books, 1993), 104.

[3] Foster Cline and Jim Fay, *Parenting With Love and Logic: Teaching Children Responsibility* (Colorado Springs, CO: Pinon Press, 1990), 34.

Session

8

Being an Encourager

Prepare for the Session

	READINGS	REFLECTIVE QUESTIONS
Monday	2 Timothy 1:6	How can you "fan into flame" the gift of God in you?
Tuesday	2 Timothy 1:7	When have you let a "spirit of timidity" creep into your life?
Wednesday	2 Timothy 1:8–12	In what circumstances have you been ashamed to be seen with other Christians?
Thursday	2 Timothy 1:13–14	How much do you depend upon the Holy Spirit to help you understand the Bible?
Friday	2 Timothy 1:15	Are there any circumstances in which you would deny Christ?
Saturday	2 Timothy 1:16–18	What believer have you "refreshed" this week?
Sunday	2 Timothy 2:1–3	What hardship have you endured as a "good soldier of Christ Jesus"?

notes:

✝

OUR GOALS FOR THIS SESSION ARE:

♾ **In groups of 6–8, gather people in a horseshoe configuration.**

Make sure everyone has a name tag.

Take time to share information on class parties that are coming up as well as any relevant church events.

BIBLE STUDY
· to learn how Paul encouraged young Timothy in the expression of his faith
· to better understand the importance of mutual encouragement in the church
· to recognize the most effective ways to encourage each other

LIFE CHANGE
· to tell each person in our families of one quality we see in him or her that gives us hope for that person's future
· to pause long enough to choose a positive reaction when people tell us their plans or dreams
· to find one person each week who is discouraged and give him or her a call

Icebreaker (10-15 minutes)

INTRODUCE THE ICEBREAKER ACTIVITY: The students have been given instructions in their books.

After the Icebreaker say something like, "Nobody likes for someone 'to rain on their parade.' That's why we need to learn to encourage, rather than discourage, each other. That will be our focus today."

Hand out the Prayer/Praise Report. A sample copy is on pages 158-159. Have people write down prayer requests and praises. Then have the prayer coordinator collect the report and make copies for use during the Caring Time.

Don't Rain on My Parade! What if your friends gave a parade in your honor? What would it be like? Fill in the following to let us know how to set it up for you.

All of the floats would be made out of:

☐ roses   ☐ chocolate
☐ orchids   ☐ Legos
☐ gold   ☐ other:_____
☐ mountain wildflowers

I would ride in:

☐ a Lexus   ☐ a stretch limo
☐ a classic Corvette   ☐ an old Model T
☐ a Cadillac   ☐ a horse-drawn carriage
☐ a giant pumpkin   ☐ other:_____
☐ a fire truck (while clanging the bell!)

The marching bands would all play:

☐ John Philip Sousa   ☐ Country hits
☐ '60s and '70s rock   ☐ Jazz pieces
☐ John Williams sound tracks

The only thing that could spoil it would be if:

☐ it rained all day
☐ my boss showed up
☐ they ran out of hot dogs and cold drinks
☐ other:_____

8

LEARNING FROM THE BIBLE

2 TIMOTHY 1:6–2:3

Have a member of the class, selected ahead of time, read the passage from 2 Timothy.

Bible Study   (30-45 minutes)

The Scripture for this week:

⁶For this reason I remind you to fan into flame the gift of God, which is in you through the laying on of my hands. ⁷For God did not give us a spirit of timidity, but a spirit of power, of love and of self-discipline.

⁸So do not be ashamed to testify about our Lord, or ashamed of me his prisoner. But join with me in suffering for the gospel, by the power of God, ⁹who has saved us and called us to a holy life—not because of anything we have done but because of his own purpose and grace. This grace was given us in Christ Jesus before the beginning of time, ¹⁰but it has now been revealed through the appearing of our Savior, Christ Jesus, who has destroyed death and has brought life and immortality to light through the gospel. ¹¹And of this gospel I was appointed a herald and an apostle and a teacher. ¹²That is why I am suffering as I am. Yet I am not ashamed, because I know whom I have believed, and am convinced that he is able to guard what I have entrusted to him for that day.

¹³What you heard from me, keep as the pattern of sound teaching, with faith and love in Christ Jesus. ¹⁴Guard the good deposit that was entrusted to you—guard it with the help of the Holy Spirit who lives in us.

¹⁵You know that everyone in the province of Asia has deserted me, including Phygelus and Hermogenes.

¹⁶May the Lord show mercy to the household of Onesiphorus, because he often refreshed me and was not ashamed of my chains. ¹⁷On the contrary, when he was in Rome, he searched hard for me until he found me. ¹⁸May the Lord grant that he will find mercy from the Lord on that day! You know very well in how many ways he helped me in Ephesus.

¹You then, my son, be strong in the grace that is in Christ Jesus. ²And the things you have heard me say in the presence of many witnesses entrust to reliable men who will also be qualified to teach others. ³Endure hardship with us like a good soldier of Christ Jesus.

notes:

Summarize these introductory remarks. Be sure to include the underlined information, which gives the answers to the student book questions (provided in the margin).

...about today's session (5 minutes)

SPEAK ENCOURAGING WORDS

A well-known song in American culture speaks of a "home on the range" where "seldom is heard a discouraging word, and the skies are not cloudy all day." Wouldn't it be great to live a life like that? Well, we can't do much about the discouraging words that come to us, any more than we can do something about cloudy days. But we can work toward having a Christian community where words of *en*couragement are an antidote to all the words of *dis*couragement that come to us from the world.

What discouraging sayings from our culture are referred to in the presentation? What others can you think of?

There are plenty of discouraging words around us. There is the message, "Nice guys finish last," that discourages us from being caring people. There is the message, "The more things change, the more they stay the same," which can discourage us from making a real, lasting difference in the world, or from making real changes in our own lives. And there is the message, "You can't fight city hall," which seeks to discourage us from political action.

Name one encouraging Scripture you heard in today's session. What other encouraging Scriptures can you think of?

Fortunately, however, there are plenty of *encouraging* words in Scripture, " 'Blessed are the meek, for they will inherit the earth' " (Matt. 5:5); " 'I am with you always, to the very end of the age' " (Matt. 28:20); and "I can do everything through him who gives me strength" (Phil. 4:13); to name a few. To really make a difference in this world, we need to take the encouraging words of the Bible and apply them as an antidote to the discouraging words of the world.

In this session, we will look at what it means to encourage those around us, whether they are non-Christians looking for a reason to hope or Christians feeling discouraged in their ministries. We will also look at the importance of such encouragement to being an effective Christian witness.

8

notes:

Remain in groups
of 6–8 people, in
a horseshoe
configuration.

**In this small-group
session, students will
be responding to the
following questions
that will help them
share their stories in
terms of Paul's words
to Timothy.**

**Have the students
explore these
questions together.**

Identifying with the Story (5-7 minutes)

1. When did you receive a note or letter of encouragement just at the time you needed it?

2. Who is the "Onesiphorus" who has stood by you and encouraged you in a time of need?

3. Which of the things that Paul writes to Timothy do you most need to encourage you in your journey at this point in time?

   ☐ *"Fan into flame the gift of God, which is in you"* (1:6)—I need to be reminded that God has given me gifts I can use.

   ☐ *"For God did not give us a spirit of timidity, but a spirit of power"* (1:7)—I need to know that when I feel timid, God is with me.

   ☐ *"This grace was given us in Christ Jesus before the beginning of time"* (1:9)—I need to know I am part of something bigger than myself, something eternal.

   ☐ *"Endure hardship with us like a good soldier of Christ Jesus."* (2:3)—I need to know that when I suffer, I don't suffer alone.

   ☐ other: _____

notes:

today's session (15-20 minutes)

Share with your class the following information which you may modify according to your own perspectives and teaching needs. The answers to the student book questions (provided in the margin) are underlined.

What professions are mentioned as particularly needing skills of encouragement?

The ability to encourage people is one of the most important skills needed throughout our society. <u>Sports coaches need it</u>. When your football team is down a couple of touchdowns at halftime, how do you inspire the team to "win one for the Gipper"? When your baseball team has lost five in a row and is now six games behind in mid-September, how do you get them to believe they can still win the pennant? <u>Teachers need it</u>. When you have a student who is burning the midnight oil to just get Cs, how do you get her to believe that her life has potential? Or for music teachers, how do you help the student who is driving his family crazy with screechy notes and discordant chords believe that one day he might play Carnegie Hall? <u>Political leaders need it</u>. When the country is in trouble, they need to help the people believe that they have "nothing to fear but fear itself."

The Need for Encouragement in the Church

It should come as no surprise then that church leaders also need this skill. In some churches, pastors look out on Sunday morning and see nothing but a smattering of gray heads. Where are the young people? In some churches people looking for volunteers are treated like phone solicitors or used-car salesmen. How do you get them to believe they are a vital part of the work of God? How do you get them to realize that God promises Christians will have victory in the end? In some churches, every proposal for a new ministry is met by far too many scowls and cold water. How do you get those making such proposals to keep a positive spirit?

The need to encourage Christian workers is certainly not new. Paul faced it as he ministered to churches experiencing various degrees of persecution, and he needed such encouragement himself when he was held for two years in a Roman jail. The encouragement he gave to Timothy is a good example of similar encouragement he gave to many other Christians. As we look at what he writes here, we find that encouragement is basically of two kinds: <u>(1) helping the person see that the challenge ahead is not as overwhelming as he or she thinks, and (2) helping the person see more clearly the power of the resources available to him or her</u>. Let's look at these two areas separately.

What two kinds of encouragement are needed by Christians?

The Challenge Ahead

What was the most intimidating challenge faced by the first-century church?

In the first-century church in which Paul and Timothy served, the most intimidating aspect of what lay ahead of them was <u>persecution</u>. Persecution had put Paul in prison. Everywhere he had preached the gospel, there were people who believed he was undermining Jewish

8

85

today's session (cont'd)

religious law and who harassed him for that reason. Sometimes the harassment was just verbal. But often it escalated to violence. Paul catalogs a variety of such episodes in 2 Corinthians 11:24–26, where he writes, "Five times I received from the Jews the forty lashes minus one. Three times I was beaten with rods, once I was stoned, three times I was shipwrecked, I spent a night and a day in the open sea, I have been constantly on the move. I have been in danger from rivers, in danger from bandits, in danger from my own countrymen, in danger from Gentiles; in danger in the city, in danger in the country, in danger at sea; and in danger from false brothers."

Paul was arrested in Jerusalem because certain religious leaders trumped up charges against him. Paul could speak authoritatively about persecution! But Paul said that, while suffering was their lot for a little while, they would eventually have the victory because of the power of Jesus. Thus Paul says in verses 8b–10, "Join with me in suffering for the gospel, by the power of God, who has saved us and called us to a holy life ... . This grace was given us in Christ Jesus before the beginning of time, but it has now been revealed through the appearing of our Savior, Christ Jesus, who has destroyed death and has brought life and immortality to light through the gospel." Now Christ did not remove death from the human experience, but he "destroyed death" by taking away death's power. If other people threatened them with death, so what? Death was just the prelude to their eternal victory! That's why Paul could urge Timothy to "Endure hardship with us like a good soldier of Christ Jesus" (2:3).

The Power Available

What two kinds of resources do we have to face challenges as Christians?

Not only was the challenge ahead of them less intimidating than others might think, but as Christians they had an abundant source of <u>internal and external resources</u> to face that challenge. Timothy's internal resources were from God and already in him. Paul likened the presence of the Holy Spirit in Timothy to a fire—a fire that was already smoldering, that could be fanned into flame. "For this reason I remind you to fan into flame the gift of God, which is in you through the laying on of my hands. For God did not give us a spirit of timidity, but a spirit of <u>power</u>, of <u>love</u> and of <u>self-discipline</u>"

As Paul told Timothy, God has given us a spirit of _____, of _____, and of _____.

(1:6–7). Paul wanted Timothy to know that when he got discouraged because of those who opposed him, like the Romans and the Jewish religious leaders, God had given him a spirit of *power* to change things.

That power built a church that has far outlived the Caesars and the old Jewish Sanhedrin. Paul also wanted Timothy to know that when he got discouraged because of the hate that met their message,

God had given him a spirit of *love*. Love ultimately wins out over hate. It did with Paul, who had started out violently persecuting the church but who was changed by the love of Christ. And finally, when Timothy got discouraged because of his own weakness, Paul wanted him to know that God had given him a spirit of *self-discipline*. Indeed, one of the toughest enemies we ever have to face is ourselves and our own inadequacies, as Paul himself confessed in Romans (Rom. 7:7–25). But spiritual disciplines like prayer, meditation, Bible study, devotion, and fasting have helped Christians through the ages to overcome human weaknesses.

Christians also have access to the external resources of which Paul reminded Timothy. A very important external resource is the support of Christian friends. Paul himself had found such support in Onesiphorus who "often refreshed him" and did some dogged detective work to find where he was imprisoned in order to support him. Few people today have heard of Onesiphorus, and yet here we learn that he played a significant role in encouraging the church's greatest evangelist. His example should say much to us about the importance of the ministry of encouragement by Christian friends.

We have some tough challenges as Christians today, even as Timothy did. But God has given us the same resources to meet those challenges: a spirit of power, love, and self-control and Christian friends who encourage us. With the resources God has given us, no challenge is too big.

One person who encouraged Paul and serves as an example to us was .

notes:

8

✝

U Remain in groups of 6–8 people, in a horseshoe configuration.

In this small-group session, students will be applying the lessons of the text to their own lives through the following questions.

The students were asked (in the student book) to choose an answer for each question and explain why.

Learning from the Story (5-7 minutes)

1. Other than yourself, who do you know who needs the kind of encouragement Paul gave Timothy? (Put names in at least two of the blanks.)

   ☐ *"Fan into flame the gift of God, which is in you"*—Someone who needs to believe in himself or herself. _____

   ☐ *"For God did not give us a spirit of timidity, but a spirit of power"*—Someone who needs to believe God can overcome his or her fears. _____

   ☐ *"This grace was given us in Christ Jesus before the beginning of time"*—Someone who needs to feel he or she is part of something eternal. _____

   ☐ *"Endure hardship with us like a good soldier of Christ."*—Someone who is going through hardship and needs to see some purpose in it. _____

2. Which of the following actions do you think have the greatest potential for encouraging other Christians?

   ☐ calling them on the phone to see how things are going
   ☐ sending them notes or emails that include uplifting Scriptures or stories
   ☐ sharing inspirational books I have read
   ☐ sharing tapes of sermons or Christian motivational speakers
   ☐ letting them know I am praying for them
   ☐ celebrating their successes
   ☐ other: _____

3. When it comes to encouraging other Christians, which of the following weather phrases best describes you?

   ☐ I'm usually "the rain on their parade."
   ☐ Well, maybe at least a "light shower on their parade."
   ☐ I'm "the cloud on their horizon"—I point out what *could* go wrong soon.
   ☐ I'm like "a partly cloudy day"—for every positive, I also point out a negative.
   ☐ I'm the "sunshine on their shoulder"—I always try to brighten people's day.
   ☐ Other:_____

life change lessons (5-7 minutes)

Share with the class the following thoughts on how the lessons of this text might be applied today. The answers to the student book questions (provided in the margin) are underlined unless the question requires a personal answer.

Why isn't accurately seeing where you are the only step you need to take to change?

If you have a tendency to be negative toward others' hopes and dreams, what is one step you can take to change that?

Accurately seeing where we are right now is always a first step to change. Some people, though, treat it like an only step. "Once I see how I am, I should just accept it—that's how I am!" But we aren't statues of stone—eternally set in one unchangeable pose. We are living, breathing, changing creatures. <u>Once we accurately see who we are, we can decide, "Is this how I want to be</u>?" If we have been "the rain on the parade" of everyone around us, or even a "partly cloudy sky," we can change to be an encourager, the "sunshine on the shoulder" of everyone we touch. How can we make that transformation? Here are some actions to get us going:

1. <u>TELL EACH PERSON IN YOUR FAMILY OF ONE QUALITY YOU SEE IN HIM OR HER THAT GIVES YOU HOPE FOR THAT PERSON'S FUTURE.</u> What gift do your family members have that they can "fan into flame"? By starting with family, we can see the effects of our encouragement on a day-to-day basis. If you don't have any family who live with you, start with a young person in your neighborhood or a coworker. Remind the person periodically of the power of his or her gift. But don't comment on how it's being used. That would make you "rain" again!

2. <u>PAUSE LONG ENOUGH TO CHOOSE A POSITIVE REACTION WHEN PEOPLE TELL YOU THEIR PLANS OR DREAMS.</u> A problem many of us have is that we react automatically. And so, if our tendency has been to be negative, we respond with why it won't work before we even think. By developing the habit of pausing, even for 30 seconds, we can take time to ask ourselves, "What can I say to encourage this person?" We don't need to lie. But there is always some way we can say, "God can make good things happen through you."

3. <u>FIND ONE PERSON EACH WEEK WHO IS DISCOURAGED AND GIVE HIM OR HER A CALL.</u> Be an Onesiphorus! Just like he searched out Paul to stand by his side, so we need to keep our eyes open for the person in need of an encouraging word. Maybe it's the person who has told the class of a struggle and suddenly stops coming. Maybe it's a person who has had a sustained health crisis, whom the class has prayed for, but whom you've not talked to. One such call might take just 5 or 10 minutes out of your week, and it can make a world of difference.

8

notes:

Caring Time (15-20 minutes)

Take this time to encourage one another in prayer. Choose two people in your church who are involved in difficult ministries and pray for the challenges they face. Pray also for the concerns listed on the Prayer/Praise Report.

Conclude your prayer time by reading together some encouraging words from Paul in Philippians 4:6–8:

> *Do not be anxious about anything, but in everything, by prayer and petition, with thanksgiving, present your requests to God. And the peace of God, which transcends all understanding, will guard your hearts and your minds in Christ Jesus.*
>
> *Finally, brothers, whatever is true, whatever is noble, whatever is right, whatever is pure, whatever is lovely, what-ever is admirable—if anything is excellent or praiseworthy—think about such things.*

⚓ CARING TIME
Remain in groups of 6–8 people, in a horseshoe configuration.

Hand out the Prayer/Praise Report to the entire group. Ask each subgroup to pray for the empty chair. Pray specifically for God to guide you to someone to bring next week to fill that chair.

After a sufficient time of prayer in subgroups, close in a corporate prayer. Say, "Next week we will talk about: 'Ministering to One Another.'"

Remind participants of the daily Scripture readings and reflective questions found on page 92.

BIBLE STUDY NOTES

Reference Notes

Use these notes to gain further understanding
of the text as you study on your own.

fan into flame. "Rekindle." Paul uses the image of a fire, not to suggest that the gift of ministry has gone out, but that it needs constant stirring so that it always burns brightly. He is also reminding Timothy of the power of the gift given him, as in the power of raging fire.
the gift of God. Paul reminds Timothy not only of his spiritual roots (the faith of his mother and grandmother), but also of the gift (*charisma* in Greek) he has been given for ministry.

Paul makes this sort of statement because Timothy is not a forceful person. *power ... love ... self-discipline.* The gift the Spirit gave Timothy leads not to timidity but to these positive characteristics.

ashamed to testify about our Lord. The gospel message about the dying Savior was not immediately popular in the first-century world. The Greeks laughed at the idea that the Messiah would die a criminal's death and that God was so weak that He would allow His own Son to die. And the Jews could not conceive of a Messiah (whom they knew to be all-powerful) dying on the cross (which they felt disqualified Him for acceptance by

2 TIMOTHY 1:6
rekindle

2 TIMOTHY 1:7
God gave us

2 TIMOTHY 1:8
the gospel

✝

2 TIMOTHY 1:8
the Gospel
(cont'd)

God). It was not easy to preach the gospel in the face of such scorn.

his prisoner. Paul may be in a Roman jail, but he knows that he is not a prisoner of Caesar. He is, and has long been, a willing prisoner of Jesus (see Eph. 3:1; 4:1; Philem. 1:9).

join with me. Rather than being ashamed of the gospel or of Paul and his suffering, Timothy ought to share in his suffering.

suffering. Paul understands from his own experience and from that of Jesus that suffering is part of what it means to follow Christ (see 3:12; Rom. 8:17; 2 Cor. 4:7–15; Phil. 1:12,29; Col. 1:24; 1 Thess. 1:6; 2:14; 3:4).

2 TIMOTHY 1:9
unmerited favor

has saved us. Timothy can face suffering because he has already experienced salvation. This is an accomplished fact.

grace. God's work of salvation depends wholly on grace (His unmerited favor lavished on His creation) not on anything we have done. This grace, which was in place from the beginning of time, is given us in Christ Jesus (see Eph. 1:4).

2 TIMOTHY 1:10
incarnation

appearing. The Greek word is *epiphaneia* (from which the English word "epiphany" is derived). It refers here to the manifestation of God's grace via the incarnation of Christ.

Savior. This was a common title in the first century. It was applied to the Roman emperor (in his role as head of the state religion) and to various gods in the mystery religions. Christians came to see that Jesus was the one and only Savior.

death ... life. Jesus' work of salvation is described in His twofold act of destroying the power of death over people (death no longer has the final word) and bringing resurrection life in its place.

2 TIMOTHY 1:12

I am not ashamed. That he is in prison brings no shame to Paul, despite how others might view it.

2 TIMOTHY 1:14

Guard the good deposit. In words paralleling verse 12 and 1 Timothy 6:20, Paul urges Timothy to preserve faithfully the "sound teaching" of the gospel.

2 TIMOTHY 1:15–17
extraordinary loyalty

Paul now gives an example of those who have deserted him. To desert him implies deserting the gospel. Then, in contrast, Paul notes the extraordinary loyalty of Onesiphorus who went out of his way to search out where Paul was being held and then to "refresh" him.

2 TIMOTHY 1:15

Asia. This refers to a province on the western side of Asia Minor, but was then a Roman province with the capital at Ephesus.

2 TIMOTHY 2:1

grace. Grace is the sphere within which the Christian lives and moves.
in Christ Jesus. The source of grace is union with Christ.

2 TIMOTHY 2:2
a trust given

Just as the gospel has been entrusted to Timothy (1:14; 1 Tim. 6:20), so he is to entrust it to others who, in turn, teach it to others. This whole process of entrusting is made doubly important by the fact that Paul will soon call Timothy to join him in Rome, implying that others will have to take over his ministry in Ephesus.

8

Session

9

Ministering to One Another

Prepare for the Session

	READINGS	REFLECTIVE QUESTIONS
Monday	Matthew 25:31–33	How much are you looking forward to Christ coming back "in his glory"?
Tuesday	Matthew 25:34	What does having a place in the kingdom mean to you?
Wednesday	Matthew 25:35–36	What have you done to minister for Christ this week?
Thursday	Matthew 25:37–39	How often do you go out of your way to help someone else?
Friday	Matthew 25:40–43	Can you remember a time when you turned your back on someone in need?
Saturday	Matthew 25:44–46	Why is it important for you to do something for "the least" in our society?
Sunday	James 2:14–17	How can you tell if your faith is alive and well?

notes:

OUR GOALS FOR THIS SESSION ARE:

⊌ In groups of 6–8, gather people in a horseshoe configuration.

Make sure everyone has a name tag.

Take time to share information on class parties that are coming up as well as any relevant church events.

INTRODUCE THE ICEBREAKER ACTIVITY: The students have been given instructions in their books.

After the Icebreaker say something like, "While we all have unique tendencies, no person is 'an island apart to himself [or herself].' The Bible affirms that truth. We are all interdependent. Today we will talk about what it means to respond to the needs of people around us."

Hand out the Prayer/Praise Report. A sample copy is on pages 158-159. Have people write down prayer requests and praises. Then have the prayer coordinator collect the report and make copies for use during the Caring Time.

BIBLE STUDY
- to sensitize ourselves to the needs around us
- to learn to see ministering to people in need as a way of loving Christ
- to explore the best ways to minister to the needs of others

LIFE CHANGE
- to make out a time-use budget, similar to a financial budget, that includes time for caring ministries
- to visit with the pastor about what he sees as caring ministries particularly suited to us
- to review caring ministries that we have committed to in other sessions of this study

Icebreaker   (10-15 minutes)

No Man Is an Island. A famous poem declares, "No man is an island, apart to himself." While that is true, some of us have sought to live an island-like lifestyle by separating ourselves from others through many ways. Which of the following land formations or natural phenomena most resemble the way you have sought to live your life?

ISLAND—I am a loner who likes my private time.

MOUNTAIN—I see myself as seeking to rise above the mediocrity around me.

ISTHMUS—I am the one who joins others together.

OASIS—I seek to be an island of life and refreshment in a dry world.

GROVE OF TREES—I live best in community.

JUNGLE—Full of life but with my dark, scary side, too.

FLOWERY MEADOW—I am colorful and inviting.

BLACKBERRY PATCH—I have good fruit, but watch my thorny side!

9

notes:

LEARNING FROM THE BIBLE

MATTHEW 25:31–46

Have a class member, selected ahead of time, read the words of the King in this parable (vv. 34b–36, 40b, 41b–43, and 45b).

Have another class member read the narration (vv. 31–34a, 37a, 40a, 41a, 44a, and 46).

Divide the rest of the class into the "sheep" who will read 37a–39 and the "goats" who will read 44b.

Bible Study (30-45 minutes)

The Scripture for this week:

³¹"When the Son of Man comes in his glory, and all the angels with him, he will sit on his throne in heavenly glory. ³²All the nations will be gathered before him, and he will separate the people one from another as a shepherd separates the sheep from the goats. ³³He will put the sheep on his right and the goats on his left.

³⁴"Then the King will say to those on his right, 'Come, you who are blessed by my Father; take your inheritance, the kingdom prepared for you since the creation of the world. ³⁵For I was hungry and you gave me something to eat, I was thirsty and you gave me something to drink, I was a stranger and you invited me in, ³⁶I needed clothes and you clothed me, I was sick and you looked after me, I was in prison and you came to visit me.'

³⁷"Then the righteous will answer him, 'Lord, when did we see you hungry and feed you, or thirsty and give you something to drink? ³⁸When did we see you a stranger and invite you in, or needing clothes and clothe you? ³⁹When did we see you sick or in prison and go to visit you?'

⁴⁰"The King will reply, 'I tell you the truth, whatever you did for one of the least of these brothers of mine, you did for me.'

⁴¹"Then he will say to those on his left, 'Depart from me, you who are cursed, into the eternal fire prepared for the devil and his angels. ⁴²For I was hungry and you gave me nothing to eat, I was thirsty and you gave me nothing to drink, ⁴³I was a stranger and you did not invite me in, I needed clothes and you did not clothe me, I was sick and in prison and you did not look after me.'

⁴⁴"They also will answer, 'Lord, when did we see you hungry or thirsty or a stranger or needing clothes or sick or in prison, and did not help you?'

⁴⁵"He will reply, 'I tell you the truth, whatever you did not do for one of the least of these, you did not do for me.'

⁴⁶"Then they will go away to eternal punishment, but the righteous to eternal life."

notes:

...about today's session (5 minutes)

WE ALL MINISTER

Summarize these introductory remarks. Be sure to include the underlined information, which gives the answers to the student book questions (provided in the margin).

We are accustomed to calling the professional clergy who lead our churches our "ministers." But many churches today affirm the fact that *all* church members are called to care for (minister to) each other. Some list in their bulletins and publications "all church members" as their ministers. This is, indeed, in accord with Scripture. In fact, many of us want to live out this designation and give of ourselves to others in a meaningful way. However, many of us also find that we have a twofold obstacle standing in the way of fulfilling our intention: (1) We don't feel we have been equipped or trained well enough to minister to others in a competent way, and (2) We don't feel we have time to take on the ministries we would like. The second drawback complicates the first because in order to feel competent to minister to others, we have to take the time to be trained. Since many of us are finding that our secular work is demanding more and more of our time, we feel we have less and less time to volunteer for church and community ministries.[1]

What twofold obstacle do many people feel stands in the way of them ministering to others?

Still, in the midst of this conflict, we need to stop and remind ourselves of the importance placed by Scripture on caring for and ministering to others. The Scripture we will be looking at this week places our ministry to others as a pivotal point in our relationship with our God. And for those of us who have known what it is like to feel hungry or alone when we were sick or a stranger, that is another factor that helps us understand the importance of ministering to each other. When we truly see this importance, then we will look at how to prioritize our time to help people in need.

What two factors help us see the importance of ministering to others?

In this session we will look at what it means to minister to other people, and we will wrestle with the practical issue of how to make time for doing so in the midst of our busy lives.

9

notes:

U Remain in groups of 6–8 people, in a horseshoe configuration.

In this small-group session, students will be responding to the following questions that will help them share their stories in terms of what Jesus says about the judgment in Matthew 25:31–46.

Have the students explore these questions together.

Identifying with the Story (5-7 minutes)

1. When did someone visit you at a time that you particularly needed it? What about that visit do you remember most?

2. Which of the areas of need that Christ mentions have you been most likely to face yourself over the course of your lifetime?

   ☐ meeting my basic needs, like putting food on the table
   ☐ meeting my social needs, like finding friends when I felt like a stranger
   ☐ affording the clothes I needed
   ☐ affording the kind of clothes I really wanted
   ☐ health needs—I've had some crises
   ☐ "prison"—finding support when I had gotten myself into trouble

3. Finish this sentence: "A time I was in need and was disappointed that more people didn't respond was when …"

notes:

today's session (15-20 minutes)

Share with your class the following information which you may modify according to your own perspectives and teaching needs. The answers to the student book questions (provided in the margin) are underlined.

In an episode of the television show, *Frasier*, Frasier and Niles invest in a development company. Unfortunately, it turns out to be the same development company that is tearing down their father Martin's favorite hang-out, "Duke's." In many respects, that scenario is similar to the truths in the Bible we're discussing today—we are inadvertently destroying what is important to our Father! By not caring when the children of our heavenly Father are going hungry, or doing without clothes, or being sick or in prison, we are contributing to their destruction.

Jesus says that those who neglect to care for the people around them, neglect to care for Him and will be judged for that neglect. Are we to take that literally? Certainly everyone has at some time or another passed by on the other side when they have seen someone in need. Wouldn't that condemn all of us? This teaching was not meant to negate the truth of <u>God's grace in Jesus Christ</u>. What it is meant to do is refocus our efforts to serve God. If we truly want to serve God, we need to do it by caring for the needs of the people around us. While we looked at this theme in session 6, we want to focus today more specifically on the kinds of needs we are called to minister to, and *how* we might minister to them.

According to the leader, the story of the sheep and the goats was not meant to negate the truth of _____.

The Needs We Must Respond To

Sometimes when we look at this story, the assumption is that we are just called to care for the "down-and-out" of society—the ones who don't have the basic necessities of life like food, shelter, and clothing. It is certainly true that we should care for such people. Jesus told a parable about caring for the poor and hungry at our gate (Luke 16:19–31), and many of the Old Testament prophets and writers spoke of the need to care for the poor (Ps. 37:14–15; Prov. 14:21,31; Isa. 1:10–17; 3:14–15; Jer. 22:15–16; Amos 2:6–7; 5:11).

However, the teaching of Jesus in Matthew 25 is really broader than that. First of all, the story specifically refers to the sick and the stranger. All of us get sick, and even the wealthiest among us can be a stranger. But even more than these specific references, the tone of this teaching is that we need to recognize and respond to the needs around us, *whatever form they take*. One way people try to ease past the implications of this story is to avoid going around the "needy neighborhoods." They think that if they just don't look at people in obvious physical need, they don't have to respond to them. They make sure they buy their homes in "nice" areas, and they go to churches in "nice" areas of town. But this is just another form of "walking by on the other side" (see Luke 10:25–37). Even more, it

9

today's session (cont'd)

Which of the needs Jesus mentions can be found in every neighborhood, regardless of its socioeconomic status?

Do you agree that "every neighborhood is a needy neighborhood"? Why or why not?

What are two approaches to helping people in need?

ignores the fact that need takes many forms. *Every* neighborhood is a needy neighborhood—the needs just take different forms in different places. <u>Loneliness</u> (feeling like a "stranger") is rampant everywhere. <u>Illness</u>, both physical and emotional, is an area of need at every socioeconomic level, and <u>family problems</u>, like divorce and discord between parents and children, infect those in the most upscale of neighborhoods. All of these needs cry out for someone willing to give a listening ear or a caring presence.

How We Care for Needs

This leads into our second area of concern: *how* to care for the needs of the people around us. There are basically two different approaches to helping people in need: <u>(1) giving them resources to meet their needs, or (2) encouraging or empowering them to meet their needs with resources they can obtain themselves.</u> Both approaches have times when they are appropriate. In times of physical need, we may just need to share our physical resources. A family has experienced a disaster like a house fire or a breadwinner who has lost a job. They don't need just kind words, they need someone who is willing to open a wallet. James writes of this in James 2:15–16, "Suppose a brother or sister is without clothes and daily food. If one of you says to him, 'Go, I wish you well; keep warm and well fed,' but does nothing about his physical needs, what good is it?" Similarly, there are even times that giving a resource can help with other kinds of needs—like giving a book of spiritual encouragement to one who is going through stress.

However, it is also true that giving someone a physical resource like money may not be the best way to help. Many of us have found this out in relationship to giving money to homeless people on the street. People become homeless for many different reasons, and some of these factors they have only minimal control over. However, abuse of drugs and/or alcohol is a factor with many of them. Giving them money can just make their need worse. Caring people need to be aware of this.

Does this mean that we just walk on by, waving them off? To do so is to ignore the fact that there are other ways to give. On one occasion when Peter and John were asked for money by a beggar with a disability, Peter responded, "Silver or gold I do not have, but what I have I give you. In the name of Jesus Christ of Nazareth, walk." They gave what they had and responded to a more basic need. Their response enabled the man to support himself. For many people on the street, their more basic need is for love and worth. Nobody takes

What can you do for a homeless person on the street if you feel that giving money may not be helpful?

time for them. Even those who do give money give it quickly and walk on. What about stopping to talk? What about showing concern? <u>One way of giving that deserves particular consideration is volunteering to take them for a meal and visiting with them while there</u>. Most people do not take time to do this, but <u>if we first take time to listen to them, telling them about Jesus can also be appropriate in this context</u>.

The Most Important Gift

What is the most important gift we can give anyone?

<u>The most important gift we can give anyone is *ourself*</u>. This is what we need to give the person who is alienated or alone. This is what we need to give to people who lose a loved one or discover they have a serious disease. We need to give of our time to listen to them and empathize with them. We need to give them our tears. We need to give them encouragement, helping them to know that they don't have to walk alone through "the valley of the shadow."

Being with someone in a time of need also encourages them to use resources they already have to meet their need. It says to them, "I know you can do it!" That's all many of us need.

Some of us would rather give money than give of ourselves—it's easier. However, Jesus doesn't call us to do what is easy. He calls us to do what is loving, and to do it as if we were doing it for Him. When we do that, we are truly blessed by our Father.

notes:

Remain in groups of 6–8 people, in a horseshoe configuration.

In this small-group session, students will be applying the lessons of the text to their own lives through the following questions.

The students were asked (in the student book) to choose an answer for each question and explain why.

✝

Learning from the Story (5-7 minutes)

1. In the family in which you grew up, which of the following phrases would have described the attitude toward people in need?

   ☐ "God helps those who help themselves."
   ☐ "Give a person a fish and he eats for a day; teach a person to fish and he eats for a lifetime."
   ☐ "If you're in need, it's probably your own fault."
   ☐ "There's always enough in our pot for one more guest."
   ☐ "It's the obligation of the privileged to share with the unfortunate."
   ☐ "It's more blessed to give than to receive."
   ☐ "There but for the grace of God go I."
   ☐ other: _____

2. If you could put a percentage on it (as they do with chances of rain) what would you say is the likelihood you refused Christ in the form of a person in need in the past week?

   ☐ less than 10 percent
   ☐ 10–25 percent
   ☐ 26–50 percent
   ☐ 51–75 percent
   ☐ 76–90 percent
   ☐ over 90 percent
   ☐ 100 percent chance!

3. What do you need to open up to in order to better live out the teaching of this passage?

   ☐ open my eyes to the needs around me
   ☐ open my wallet a little more
   ☐ open my mind and stop being so judgmental
   ☐ open my schedule so I can spend more time visiting
   ☐ open up to more effective ways of helping than just doling out spare change
   ☐ other: _____

notes:

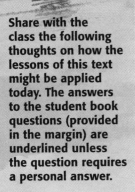

life change lessons (5-7 minutes)

Share with the class the following thoughts on how the lessons of this text might be applied today. The answers to the student book questions (provided in the margin) are underlined unless the question requires a personal answer.

Ministering to others can be a hard thing to put into action because it takes *time*. But God calls us to be good managers of all we have, including our time. While it is too much to expect that we will spend all of our free time helping others, we certainly ought to budget a portion of our time for that purpose. There is no legalistic formula for this. Rather, we should take it to God, seeking His guidance on what is best. Some people might give at least 10 percent of their non-work hours like they give at least 10 percent of their money. Others might dedicate a certain number of evenings or Saturdays a month to caring ministries. For others, their caring ministry might take just a few well-placed minutes a day and yet have great effect. In any case, caring for others in the name of Christ should be a high priority for the Christian who wants to reach higher in their spiritual journey. Some specific steps we might try include:

What kind of budget does the leader advise you to use?

1. MAKE OUT A <u>TIME-USE</u> BUDGET, SIMILAR TO A FINANCIAL BUDGET, THAT INCLUDES TIME FOR CARING MINISTRIES. This is a good life discipline for anyone. But for a busy Christian trying to figure out how to find time for a caring ministry, it is vital. Include time estimates on all the essentials of living (eating, sleeping, hygiene, working, and driving to work), as well as family time, recreational time, devotional time, self-improvement, exercise, etc. You might start by recording how much time you actually spend on all these activities during one week. Then the next week, make out a budget according to how you feel you *ought* to be spending your time.

What else can help you decide which caring ministry to get involved in?

2. <u>ASK YOUR PASTOR WHAT CARING MINISTRIES MIGHT BE PARTICULARLY SUITED FOR YOU.</u> If you have taken a spiritual gifts course, such as the one Serendipity has in this series (*Unique Design*), refer to that to refresh your mind on what gifts you could apply to caring ministry. Use this information to focus on a caring ministry best suited to you.

9

3. <u>REVIEW CARING MINISTRIES THAT YOU HAVE COMMITTED TO IN OTHER SESSIONS OF THIS STUDY.</u> Particular caring ministries were suggested in several of the previous sessions, including session 4 (life change goal 3), session 6 (life change goal 2) and session 8 (life change goal 3). Maintain these and include them in your time-use budget.

notes:

Caring Time (15-20 minutes)

CARING TIME
Remain in groups of 6–8 people, in a horseshoe configuration.

Hand out the Prayer/Praise Report to the entire group. Ask each subgroup to pray for the empty chair. Pray specifically for God to guide you to someone to bring next week to fill that chair.

After a sufficient time of prayer in subgroups, close in a corporate prayer. Say, "Next week we will talk about: 'Building Relationships with Unchurched Friends.' "

Remind participants of the daily Scripture readings and reflective questions found on page 104.

Use this time to pray for one another, remembering the needs expressed in question 3 under "Learning from the Story." Have each person in your group pray for one area of need in your community (homelessness, drug addiction, loneliness of the elderly, etc.). Also, use the Prayer/Praise Report and pray for the concerns listed.

 notes:

BIBLE STUDY NOTES

MATTHEW 25:31
a throne

MATTHEW 25:32
universal judgement

MATTHEW 25:34
Son of Man

Reference Notes

Use these notes to gain further understanding
of the text as you study on your own.

he will sit on his throne. Because the Son of Man is sitting on His throne, the implication is that there will be a judgment.

All the nations. This is a universal, worldwide judgment. While modern use of the word "nation" typically implies a political entity, here it refers to the various races and ethnic groups. All people will be present at this judgment scene.

separates the sheep from the goats. These animals grazed in common herds during the day. At night, however, they were separated because the goats needed to be in shelters to be protected from the elements.

In this verse, the Son of Man (v. 31) is clearly identified as God's Son and the King of God's kingdom.

you who are blessed. The Beatitudes (Matt. 5:3–12) outline the qualities of those people who receive God's favor.

prepared for you since the creation of the world. Contrast this with the punishment of the wicked in the eternal fire "prepared for the devil and his angels" (v. 41). What God has intended and prepared for all people is the loving fellowship of His kingdom. People were not made for destruction although some choose it by rejecting Jesus as Savior. The place of eternal destruction was made for the devil and his angels. That the kingdom was prepared "since the creation of the world" for the righteous means that

MATTHEW 25:34
Son of Man (cont'd)

MATTHEW 25:35
a virtue

MATTHEW 25:36
prisoners

MATTHEW 25:37
a righteous act

MATTHEW 25:40
brothers of Christ

MATTHEW 25:41
eternal fire

MATTHEW 25:44
love of God

MATTHEW 25:45
do good

God's original intent was for people to share in His eternal kingdom of love and justice.

I was a stranger. Hospitality to strangers was a highly regarded virtue in ancient Israel. The story of Lot and Sodom reinforced this virtue of hospitality to strangers (Gen. 19:1–26).

in prison. Probably those (like John the Baptist) who were in prison because they resisted the state out of faithfulness to God are in view. Visiting such a prisoner would put the visitor at risk since he or she might be identified as a sympathizer. It may also simply reflect the fact that many people were in prison because of their inability to pay off a debt. Hence, these too are the poor.

Lord, when did we see you? The righteous did not act in this way because they had some type of insight regarding the spirit of Christ in the poor. They simply acted with compassion toward those in need.

Just as Jesus served the poor and needy (both in a physical and spiritual sense), so He asserts that acts of mercy for the poor and needy are the way He is served in this world.

these brothers of mine. While it is uncertain whether this phrase actually is meant to reflect Christ's solidarity with all the poor or only with those who bear His name, such a debate may be akin to the question of the lawyer regarding just who was really his neighbor (Luke 10:29–37). The point is that the righteous are those who have a heart of compassion for all in need.

The cursed are those who show a lack of concern for the needs of others. *the eternal fire.* The idea of hell, a place of eternal punishment by fire, reflects Israel's experience with the valley of *Gehenna*, a ravine outside Jerusalem where children were once sacrificed to the god Molech (1 Kings 11:7). Jews considered it a defiled place, good only as a garbage dump that burned continually. *Gehenna* became a symbol for the place of punishment and spiritual death.
prepared for the devil and his angels. The Bible tells us that Satan led a rebellion of angels against God, and they were all condemned for it (see Isa. 14:11–15; 2 Peter 2:4; Rev. 19:20; 20:10).

Lord, when did we see you? With this teaching Jesus condemned those who look past the suffering of the world as they seek a detached religiosity. The New Testament is consistent in saying that love of God and love of people, especially people in need, must go together (see Matt. 22:34–40; Jas. 2:14–17; 1 John 2:9–11; 4:7–12,19–20).

whatever you did not do. It is not enough simply to avoid doing bad things—people will be judged also for the good things they neglected to do. All can appeal to the grace of God in Jesus Christ, certainly, but the fact remains that God's expectation is that His children will do good as well as avoid doing bad.

To check on current trends in volunteer time see the current issue of George Barna, *What Americans Believe: An Annual Survey of Values and Religious Views in the United States* (Ventura, CA: Regal Books).

Session

10

Building Relationships with Unchurched Friends

Prepare for the Session

	READINGS	REFLECTIVE QUESTIONS
Monday	John 4:4–9	What causes you to avoid someone? How can you treat others as Jesus did?
Tuesday	John 4:10–14	Have you drunk the living water Christ offers? How does your life reflect "a spring of water welling up to eternal life"?
Wednesday	John 4:15–18	How honest are you with God about your life—your sin?
Thursday	John 4:19–24	What helps you worship God in spirit and in truth?
Friday	John 4:25–29	Who have you told that Jesus is the Christ? What is your biggest obstacle in telling others about Christ?
Saturday	Luke 19:1–10	How do you feel about associating with unbelievers? What does Jesus' example teach you?
Sunday	Luke 7:36–50	How deeply do you love God? Take some time to thank Him for the great debt His Son paid for you.

notes:

OUR GOALS FOR THIS SESSION ARE:

☖ **In groups of 6–8, gather people in a horseshoe configuration.**

Make sure everyone has a name tag.

Take time to share information on class parties that are coming up as well as any relevant church events.

INTRODUCE THE ICEBREAKER ACTIVITY: The students have been given instructions in their books.

After the Icebreaker say something like, "People can be defensive of their 'holy places' as we will see in our Scripture today. But as Christians, our task is to convince the unsaved of the worth of a *person* (Christ), not a *place* (our church buildings). Today, we will look at how to reach out in the name of Christ to those who don't always enjoy 'holy places.' "

Hand out the Prayer/Praise Report. A sample copy is on pages 158-159. Have people write down prayer requests and praises. Then have the prayer coordinator collect the report and make copies for use during the Caring Time.

✚ **BIBLE STUDY**
- to learn how Jesus related to people who were not traditionally "religious"
- to understand the importance of developing friendships with those outside the church
- to know how to show caring for unchurched people

LIFE CHANGE
- to evaluate our present friendship patterns
- to focus on developing or strengthening a friendship with a person who doesn't attend church
- to ask an unchurched friend about what he or she believes or values

Icebreaker   (10-15 minutes)

My Holy Places. In biblical times, there were a variety of places that were considered "holy places." What places are the closest to being "holy places" for you—places that you feel at peace in your spirit or feel close to God?

- ☐ a special place I go in the mountains
- ☐ my favorite fishing hole
- ☐ Do golf courses count?
- ☐ at the home of some close friends where we have had many spiritual discussions far into the evening
- ☐ a place I go in the country
- ☐ a little roadside chapel
- ☐ the place where I was saved
- ☐ the sanctuary where I was married
- ☐ other: _____

notes:

10

LEARNING FROM THE BIBLE

JOHN 4:4–29

Select three class members ahead of time to read this story: One to read the words of Jesus, one to read the words of the woman, and one to read the narration.

Bible Study   (30-45 minutes)

The Scripture for this week:

⁴He [Jesus] had to go through Samaria. ⁵So he came to a town in Samaria called Sychar, near the plot of ground Jacob had given to his son Joseph. ⁶Jacob's well was there, and Jesus, tired as he was from the journey, sat down by the well. It was about the sixth hour.

⁷When a Samaritan woman came to draw water, Jesus said to her, "Will you give me a drink?" ⁸(His disciples had gone into the town to buy food.)

⁹The Samaritan woman said to him, "You are a Jew and I am a Samaritan woman. How can you ask me for a drink?" (For Jews do not associate with Samaritans.)

¹⁰Jesus answered her, "If you knew the gift of God and who it is that asks you for a drink, you would have asked him and he would have given you living water."

¹¹"Sir," the woman said, "you have nothing to draw with and the well is deep. Where can you get this living water? ¹²Are you greater than our father Jacob, who gave us the well and drank from it himself, as did also his sons and his flocks and herds?"

¹³Jesus answered, "Everyone who drinks this water will be thirsty again, ¹⁴but whoever drinks the water I give him will never thirst. Indeed, the water I give him will become in him a spring of water welling up to eternal life."

¹⁵The woman said to him, "Sir, give me this water so that I won't get thirsty and have to keep coming here to draw water."

¹⁶He told her, "Go, call your husband and come back."

¹⁷"I have no husband," she replied. Jesus said to her, "You are right when you say you have no husband. ¹⁸The fact is, you have had five husbands, and the man you now have is not your husband. What you have just said is quite true."

¹⁹"Sir," the woman said, "I can see that you are a prophet. ²⁰Our fathers worshiped on this mountain, but you Jews claim that the place where we must worship is in Jerusalem."

²¹Jesus declared, "Believe me, woman, a time is coming when you will worship the Father neither on this mountain nor in Jerusalem. ²²You Samaritans worship what you do not know; we worship what we do know, for salvation is from the Jews. ²³Yet a time is coming and has now come when the true worshipers will worship the Father in spirit and truth, for they are the kind of worshipers the Father seeks. ²⁴God is spirit, and his worshipers must worship in spirit and in truth."

✝

²⁵The woman said, "I know that Messiah" (called Christ) "is coming. When he comes, he will explain everything to us."

²⁶Then Jesus declared, "I who speak to you am he."

²⁷Just then his disciples returned and were surprised to find him talking with a woman. But no one asked, "What do you want?" or "Why are you talking with her?"

²⁸Then, leaving her water jar, the woman went back to the town and said to the people, ²⁹"Come, see a man who told me everything I ever did. Could this be the Christ?"

notes:

Summarize these introductory remarks. Be sure to include the underlined information, which gives the answers to the student book questions (provided in the margin).

What percentage of people in the United States claim to be in church on any given Sunday?

Where did Jesus most often meet with people? Who was He most likely to be with?

...about today's session (5 minutes)

IN THE FOOTSTEPS OF CHRIST

About 44 percent of the American people claim to be in church on any given Sunday.¹ But who is sharing the story of Jesus' transforming power with that other 56 percent? Certainly some of these come into the church on occasion, but many have never darkened the doors of a church building. Many churches are trying everything from mass mailings to media advertising to need-focused programming to bring them in, but still most resist. What do we do? We follow Jesus' example: since we can't get them to church, we take the church to them!

Jesus did not spend much of His ministry preaching in the buildings devoted to religious worship. When He read Scripture related to His mission in the synagogue at Nazareth (Luke 4:16–30), that was the exception rather than the rule. He met people where they lived. He spoke to them of hope and good news while they were in the midst of their day-to-day routines. His companions were more likely to be the "unchurched" of His day: tax-collectors, prostitutes, and poor working people.

10

about today's session (cont'd)

In contrast, many church-goers today confess to having few if any friends outside the church. When asked to bring their friends to church, they will say something like, "But all of my friends *already* go to church." How can we serve as ambassadors of Christ to unchurched people if we don't know them? Let's be careful to understand that this does not mean we should *act like* friends in order to manipulate them into going to church or making a faith decision. We need to genuinely be their friend—listening to them and being there for them in their times of need. Then we can tell them how to begin a relationship with Jesus when the appropriate opportunity comes. In that way, we can truly walk in the footsteps of Jesus Christ.

notes:

♘ Remain in groups of 6–8 people, in a horseshoe configuration.

In this small-group session, students will be responding to the following questions that will help them share their stories in terms of Jesus' interaction with the woman from Samaria in John 4:4–29.

Have the students explore these questions together.

✝ Identifying with the Story (5-7 minutes)

1. Where was the most popular "watering hole" (the place where everyone gathered for refreshment and conversation) when you were a teenager?

2. What group were you not supposed to talk to or socialize with in your teen years?

   ☐ the druggies
   ☐ people of another race
   ☐ non-church kids
   ☐ kids who smoked
   ☐ those "on the other side of the track"
   ☐ none of these—we could speak with anyone!

✝

3. What was it that you most "thirsted for" during your adolescence?

- ☐ attention from the opposite sex
- ☐ respect and recognition for my achievements
- ☐ truly intimate friendship
- ☐ my parent(s) attention
- ☐ a place to belong
- ☐ forgiveness
- ☐ love
- ☐ other: _____

notes:

Share with your class the following information which you may modify according to your own perspectives and teaching needs. The answers to the student book questions (provided in the margin) are underlined.

Why did the Jews look down upon Samaritans?

today's session (15-20 minutes)

The woman in this story was the "lowest of the low" according to the Jewish social hierarchy of the day. She was first of all a Samaritan, a cultural group the Jews despised. The Samaritan people came into being after Assyria defeated the northern tribes of Israel in 722 B.C. The Assyrians carried Israel's most prominent citizens into exile in their own country. These tribes have been lost to history. However, they left the lowest members of the Jewish society in the land and sent their own people to intermarry with them. The result was a group that was a half-breed of hated foreigners and Jewish social rejects. Making this worse in the eyes of the pious Jews in the country of Judah to the south was the fact that the Assyrians who immigrated brought their religion with them. This aggravated some religious differences that already existed between the people of the north (who worshiped in a variety of local shrines connected with the patriarchs), and the people of Judah who said all worship should be done in the temple in Jerusalem.

10

today's session (cont'd)

So the person Jesus encountered at Sychar was a Samaritan and bad in the eyes of Jewish tradition. That she was also a *woman* made her even lower. The pious Jewish male would pray, "Lord, I thank you that you did not make me a Gentile, a slave, or a woman." Women were not thought worthy to be taught the religious literature of Judaism. One rabbinical saying was that it is better for a father to teach his daughter lechery than to teach her the Law. When Jesus told His story about the man who was a neighbor to the man who fell among thieves, He made the hero a Samaritan, which scandalized the pious Jews. But what He did at Sychar was even more scandalous because He showed courtesy and respect to a Samaritan woman who was living in sin. One wonders how scandalized people would have been had He made the hero of the Good Samaritan story a Samaritan woman!

What is the probable reason why this woman came for water at noon?

In addition to the Jews who would not talk to her, this woman probably also had a lot of Samaritans in her own town who wouldn't talk to her. She had been married five times and now had pretty much given up on "respectable life" by living with a man outside of wedlock. "Respectable" women wouldn't talk *to* her—however, they probably couldn't wait to talk *about* her, as her life was doubtlessly fodder for gossip. This may be why she came for water in the heat of the noonday sun, when other women wouldn't be there.

Jesus' Loving Action

In the midst of all these negative things about this woman, Jesus spoke to her with the same respect He spoke to anyone else. He even asked her to let Him have a drink from the same cup she was using herself. (Bill Cosby used to have a comedy routine about his childhood where in trying to show friendship to another kid he let him drink from the same soda pop bottle and he wouldn't even wipe off the mouth of the bottle—that was friendship!) Jesus also answered her questions, offering her hope that her life could be turned around, and that she could find "a spring of water welling up to eternal life." That was probably the best thing of all for someone everyone else turned their backs on.

What was probably "the best thing of all" that Jesus did in responding to this woman?

Befriending the Unchurched

Now, in applying the lesson, we don't want to make the mistake of over-identifying this woman with today's unchurched person. Many people who don't go to church live very respectable lives and have solid, faithful marriages. However, many in the church relate to unchurched people like most people related to this Samaritan woman. We were told way back in childhood that "bad company

110

ruins good morals." What's more, we don't want to hang around with anyone who might question our beliefs. That might make others question our faith. So we keep our distance from the unchurched person. Of course, this is even more the case with unchurched people who are involved in morally incorrect practices such as homosexual activity, adulterous relationships, abortion, gossip, etc.

How did Jesus respond when the disciples returned and found Him talking to a Samaritan woman?

It is significant that Jesus never seemed to worry too much about what people might think. When the disciples returned and found Him talking with a Samaritan woman, Jesus didn't even feel obligated to explain what He was doing or defend Himself. And apparently they knew better than to ask (v. 27). In another situation, He allowed a woman of ill-repute to anoint His feet with her tears, and dry them with her hair (Luke 7:36–50). Jesus was not afraid to befriend sinners. He even had dinner with a hated tax collector (Luke 19:1–10).

None of this is to say that Christians shouldn't use discretion in their social contacts. A man who repeatedly visits one-on-one with a promiscuous woman "to show her Christian friendship" is playing with fire. But such a visit *could* be made by a woman or a couple.

Lessons from Jesus

What three lessons do we learn from Jesus' interaction with this woman?

There are at least three lessons we can learn from Jesus' inter-action with this woman, about how to build relationships with unchurched friends: (1) *Take time to listen to them*. Don't assume you know how they think and feel based on stereotypes. Jesus did not let the cultural bias against Samaritans dictate His interaction, and we shouldn't either. Some might assume, for instance, that unchurched people don't believe in God, and that's not always true. Sometimes what they don't believe in is the church! Sometimes their concept of God is far different than that of traditional Christianity, and sometimes they don't believe in God, but knowing where they are on this requires listening. (2) *Don't be defensive about their questions*. Jesus let the Samaritan woman question the Jewish tradition of temple worship in Jerusalem. That was a very emotional issue for a Jew, but Jesus always valued people over cultural tradition. Unchurched people might question anything from the goodness of God to the uniqueness of Jesus Christ to the need for the institutional church. Listening to such questions without being defensive helps the person know that you value their perspectives. It also shows the person that you have a strong enough faith to let it stand without constantly feeling a need to defend it. There can be no dumb questions and no off-limits questions. (3) *Remember that true friendship is between equals and involves giving and receiving*. Jesus started His interaction with this woman by asking her for a drink of water. While He was thirsty, Jesus also recognized that in a true relationship, people need to give as well as receive. If a

10

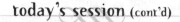

today's session (cont'd)

relationship is all a case of you giving and me receiving, I'm going to feel like the inferior, dependent partner. Most people don't like that feeling, and they don't trust relationships that take on that nature. By encouraging the woman to give to Him, He showed that He didn't feel superior to her, and He made her more receptive to receiving what He had to give. So, as we develop friendships with unchurched people, we need to open ourselves up to receiving what they have to give, as well as being willing to give them what we have.

That some people won't come to church, then, need not limit us in our outreach efforts. If we are willing to take the approach of Jesus, and be caring friends to the unchurched, we *can* take the church to them.

Remain in groups of 6–8 people, in a horseshoe configuration.

In this small-group session, students will be applying the lessons of the text to their own lives through the following questions.

The students were asked (in the student book) to choose an answer for each question and explain why.

Learning from the Story (5-7 minutes)

1. If you were to encounter Jesus face-to-face, as this woman did, what one question would you most want to ask Him?

2. Of the things Jesus did in this encounter, which one would impress you the most had you been the woman at the well?

   ☐ just talking to me at all, when it wasn't socially acceptable
   ☐ not taking sides in the religious/cultural dispute over where one was to worship
   ☐ His knowledge of my past
   ☐ His acceptance of me in spite of my past

3. How do you react when someone finds you doing something that is not acceptable in your culture, as Jesus was by talking to a Samaritan woman?

   ☐ I try to justify my actions.
   ☐ I do what I think is right and don't worry about others' reactions.
   ☐ I'm careful to never do anything not approved of in my culture.
   ☐ I just pretend it didn't happen.
   ☐ I get angry at their narrow-mindedness.
   ☐ other:_____

life change lessons (5-7 minutes)

Share with the class the following thoughts on how the lessons of this text might be applied today. The answers to the student book questions (provided in the margin) are underlined unless the question requires a personal answer.

For too many Christians, evangelism only happens in these two places:

For too many Christians in our world, telling others about the mercy and forgiveness that God offers happens in only two places: <u>church worship services and evangelistic meetings such as with Billy Graham or Luis Palau</u>. But most of the unchurched people of our culture, the ones who need the good news of Jesus Christ the most will seldom frequent such places. They may only hear the good news about Jesus if a friend shares it with them where they live or work. That is why we need to learn to be such a friend. Here are some concrete steps we can take to move in that direction:

1. EVALUATE YOUR PRESENT FRIENDSHIP PATTERNS. How many of your friends attend church and how many are unchurched? Are the unchurched people you know friends or just nodding acquaintances? Think through how you can benefit from developing other friendships, especially with people who are unchurched. Acknowledge the fears you might have about being with people who think differently than you about matters of faith.

What can you do in order to develop or strengthen a friendship with an unchurched person?

2. FOCUS IN THE NEXT WEEK ON DEVELOPING OR STRENGTHENING A FRIENDSHIP WITH A PERSON WHO DOESN'T ATTEND CHURCH. <u>Find someone with whom you have something in common</u>—an interest in sports, a hobby, children who attend the same school as yours, etc. Call this person on the phone or invite him or her over. <u>Talk about that common interest</u>. Take time to listen to the person and show your respect for their opinion. Don't initiate any discussions on religion, at least not in the first visit together. Just learn about this person and find what there is about him or her that you can appreciate and even treasure.

3. ASK AN UNCHURCHED FRIEND WHAT HE OR SHE BELIEVES OR VALUES. <u>Find out what this friend values or believes that you also value and believe</u>. *Don't* use this as an excuse to share what you believe as that might feel like manipulation. Rather, use it to just listen. Do any of his or her beliefs surprise you? Are any of them different than the stereotype church people might have? <u>If you do a good job of listening and showing interest in this person's ideas, you will have plenty of opportunities to share what you believe later</u>.

10

notes:

CARING TIME
Remain in groups of 6–8 people, in a horseshoe configuration.

Hand out the Prayer/Praise Report to the entire group. Ask each subgroup to pray for the empty chair. Pray specifically for God to guide you to someone to bring next week to fill that chair.

After a sufficient time of prayer in subgroups, close in a corporate prayer. Say, "Next week we will talk about: 'Sharing My Faith.' "

Remind participants of the daily Scripture readings and reflective questions found on page 116.

Caring Time (15-20 minutes)

Close by sharing prayer requests and praying for one another. Have each person in your group share the name of an unchurched friend or acquaintance and something about that person. Then pray for the people named. In addition, pray for the concerns on the Prayer/Praise Report.

notes:

BIBLE STUDY NOTES

Reference Notes

Use these notes to gain further understanding
of the text as you study on your own.

JOHN 4:4
Samaritans

he had to go. Probably prompted by the suspicion His popularity aroused. *Samaria.* A territory sandwiched between the Jewish provinces of Judea and Galilee. Samaritans were a race of mixed Jewish and Gentile parentage. In Jesus' day, strict Jews (who considered Samaritans religious half-breeds), would go miles out of their way to avoid Samaria entirely by crossing the Jordan River and traveling on its east side.

JOHN 4:5

the plot of ground. Genesis 48:22 tells of Jacob having given some land to his son, Joseph.

JOHN 4:7
a woman

a Samaritan woman. Not only were Samaritans despised, women were considered to be of much less value than men. A traditional rabbi would not teach women. In addition to this lower status of women, we find that this woman is living an immoral life.

came to draw water. Noontime, during the heat of the day, was not the time women would normally perform this chore. This woman probably came at this time to avoid meeting up with the "more respectable women."

✝

JOHN 4:9
a request

Jews do not associate. A "good Jew" would not use the same cup or bucket such a person was using. Jesus' request shocks the woman. Her response may well be mixed with more than a touch of sarcasm.

JOHN 4:10
living water

living water. This was a common phrase meaning water that flowed from a river or spring. Water like this had better quality than the standing water of a well or pond. Jesus, however, is referring to spiritually "living water"— water that refreshes the soul.

JOHN 4:13–14
thirst no more

will be thirsty again … will never thirst. In contrast to physical water, which quenches the thirst only for awhile, what Jesus gives will quench the spiritual thirst of people, permanently filling their need. In Matthew 5:6 Jesus said, "Blessed are those who hunger and thirst for righteousness, for they will be filled."

JOHN 4:17–18

While clearly revealing His knowledge of her situation, Jesus commends her truthfulness. Women at this time could be divorced for trivial reasons but had no right to divorce their husbands.

JOHN 4:20
tradition

mountain. This issue was a source of great hostility between Jews and Samaritans. Jewish zealots had destroyed the Samaritan temple at Mt. Gerizim many years before, and Samaritans had, at times, retaliated by desecrating the Jerusalem temple. See Deuteronomy 11:29 and Judges 9:7 as examples of worship on Mt. Gerizim. The woman may have been referring to this conflict to see whose "side" Jesus was on, and whether He would really speak to Samaritans.

JOHN 4:21
culture

neither on this mountain. By this pronouncement Jesus refuses to take sides in a cultural argument. Rather, He seeks to point to the fact that it is the spirit with which one worships that matters.

JOHN 4:25
Messiah

Messiah. The Samaritan's concept of the Messiah (based on Deut. 18:18) was less politically charged than that of the Jews. To the Samaritans, the Messiah was the One who would restore true worship and teach as Moses had done. Given this contrast, Jesus could affirm this title for Himself without fear of its being misinterpreted in political terms.

JOHN 4:27
taboo

talking with a woman. One rabbinical saying cautioned a rabbi against talking even with his wife in public on account of what others, not knowing she was his wife, might say. The concern was not just with the rabbi's reputation, but with the fact that women were thought unworthy to be taught God's Law.

10

notes:

---

[1] From a web site of the University of Michigan, U-M News and Information Services at *www.umich.edu/newsinfo/Releases/1997/Dec97/r121097a.html.*

Session

11

Sharing My Faith

Prepare for the Session

	READINGS	REFLECTIVE QUESTIONS
Monday	Acts 8:26	When have you felt the Holy Spirit guiding you in your life?
Tuesday	Acts 8:27–31	Do you understand the Bible well enough to explain it to someone who's interested in Christ? Why or why not?
Wednesday	Acts 8:32–35	To whom have you explained the good news of Jesus?
Thursday	Acts 8:36–40	When was the last time you went on your way rejoicing because of God's grace and forgiveness in your life?
Friday	Matthew 5:6	How much do you hunger and thirst for righteousness?
Saturday	Isaiah 53:1–7	Consider for a few moments the price that Christ paid for you.
Sunday	Matthew 13:1–23	What could you do to improve the spiritual soil of your life?

notes:

OUR GOALS FOR THIS SESSION ARE:

◡ In groups of 6–8, gather people in a horseshoe configuration.

Make sure everyone has a name tag.

Take time to share information on class parties that are coming up as well as any relevant church events.

BIBLE STUDY

- to learn how Philip shared his faith with the Ethiopian eunuch
- to learn some effective methods used in the Bible for sharing faith
- to consider the Holy Spirit's role in our faith-sharing

LIFE CHANGE

- to pray daily for God to guide us to receptive people
- to pray for three or four days, then make a list of people we believe God is leading us to speak to
- to review our spiritual stories we wrote out in session 1
- to witness to at least one person this week

Icebreaker (10-15 minutes)

INTRODUCE THE ICEBREAKER ACTIVITY: The students have been given instructions in their books.

After the Icebreaker say something like, "All Christians are called to be part of a harvest—a harvest of souls for Jesus Christ. The results of this spiritual harvest will vary. In this session we will talk about some biblical attitudes and skills that help us share our faith and maximize the harvest of souls we are called to be part of."

Hand out the Prayer/Praise Report. A sample copy is on pages 158-159. Have people write down prayer requests and praises. Then have the prayer coordinator collect the report and make copies for use during the Caring Time.

This Week's Harvest. If you were to describe what you feel you have "harvested" or accomplished this past week, what kind of harvest would it be?

- ☐ back to "dust bowl" days—not a plant in sight has survived
- ☐ some shriveled fruit—enough to stave off starvation
- ☐ a below-average crop—nothing to be proud of
- ☐ an average crop—there are some successes I could point out
- ☐ an above-average crop—there are many successes I could point out
- ☐ a bumper crop—everything I touched thrived

notes:

11

**LEARNING FROM
THE BIBLE**

ACTS 8:26–40

**Have two members
of the class, selected
ahead of time, read
the story of Philip
and the Ethiopian
eunuch in Acts.
One should read the
eunuch's words and
the other read the
narration and
Philip's words.**

Bible Study (30-45 minutes)

The Scripture for this week:

²⁶*An angel of the Lord said to Philip, "Go south to the road—the desert road—that goes down from Jerusalem to Gaza."* ²⁷*So he started out, and on his way he met an Ethiopian eunuch, an important official in charge of all the treasury of Candace, queen of the Ethiopians. This man had gone to Jerusalem to worship,* ²⁸*and on his way home was sitting in his chariot reading the book of Isaiah the prophet.* ²⁹*The Spirit told Philip, "Go to that chariot and stay near it."*

³⁰*Then Philip ran up to the chariot and heard the man reading Isaiah the prophet. "Do you understand what you are reading?" Philip asked.*

³¹*"How can I," he said, "unless someone explains it to me?" So he invited Philip to come up and sit with him.*

³²*The eunuch was reading this passage of Scripture:*

"He was led like a sheep to the slaughter,
and as a lamb before the shearer is silent,
so he did not open his mouth.
33In his humiliation he was deprived of justice.
Who can speak of his descendants?
For his life was taken from the earth."

³⁴*The eunuch asked Philip, "Tell me, please, who is the prophet talking about, himself or someone else?"* ³⁵*Then Philip began with that very passage of Scripture and told him the good news about Jesus.*

³⁶*As they traveled along the road, they came to some water and the eunuch said, "Look, here is water. Why shouldn't I be baptized?"* ³⁸*And he gave orders to stop the chariot. Then both Philip and the eunuch went down into the water and Philip baptized him.* ³⁹*When they came up out of the water, the Spirit of the Lord suddenly took Philip away, and the eunuch did not see him again, but went on his way rejoicing.* ⁴⁰*Philip, however, appeared at Azotus and traveled about, preaching the gospel in all the towns until he reached Caesarea.*

...about today's session (5 minutes)

FAITH-SHARERS

Summarize these introductory remarks. Be sure to include the underlined information, which gives the answers to the student book questions (provided in the margin).

What percentage of people did George Barna find believe strongly in sharing their faith, and what percentage did he find strongly believe they have no such responsibility?

What percentage of adults in the United States did George Barna find agreed with the statement that when another person tries to explain their religious beliefs, it is "usually annoying"?

According to a George Barna study, Americans are deeply divided on the issue of whether a person should share his or her religious faith. A little over one-fourth of all adults <u>(28 percent) strongly believe that they have a responsibility to share their faith with others</u>. An equivalent proportion of adults <u>(25 percent) feel equally strongly that they do not have any such responsibility</u>. The rest of the population is caught somewhere in the middle on this issue.[1] In another Barna study, nearly half of the population <u>(42 percent) said that when another person tries to explain their religious beliefs, it is "usually annoying."</u>[2] Why are we so deeply divided? Why is it "annoying"?

Perhaps it is because so many people who have shared their faith have done so without tact and often without the love that is to be at the heart of that sharing. Many feel that they are being accosted on the streets and in their homes by people who will neither listen nor take "no" for an answer. Such faith-sharers are put into the same category with the sleaziest kind of salesmen, and many feel that if that is what it means to share their faith, they want no part of it.

Still, Christ calls us to share our faith. We are to go into all the world to preach the gospel (Matt. 28:19), and we are to be His witnesses "to the ends of the earth" (Acts 1:8). And if we truly believe that Christ has made a difference for eternity in our lives, shouldn't we say something about Him to a world that is full of stress and spiritual confusion?

The key is how we share and what our motivation is. If our motivation is simply to gain some kind of credit for ourselves or to act like someone with all the answers, people will sense that and despise our message. But if we are motivated by love for the people around us and a conviction that Christ is the only way to obtain forgiveness for our sins and live eternally in heaven, then our message might find a more receptive audience—and, equally important, we will feel better about sharing it. Learning how to share faith in this caring way is what this session is all about.

notes:

11

✝

Remain in groups of 6–8 people, in a horseshoe configuration.

In this small-group session, students will be responding to the following questions.

Have the students explore these questions together.

Identifying with the Story (5-7 minutes)

1. Finish this sentence with one of the choices that follow: "A time in my life when, like the Ethiopian eunuch, I was really searching for spiritual answers was …"

   ☐ in college, when truth seemed up for grabs
   ☐ when a loved one died
   ☐ when I reached the top rung on the ladder and realized it was empty
   ☐ when I left home for the first time and experienced the diversity of the world
   ☐ when I reached midlife and was re-evaluating what it was all about
   ☐ right now
   ☐ that has never happened to me

2. A person who, like Philip, came alongside me in my journey and provided some insights was:

3. Compare your own coming to Christ with the Ethiopian eunuch, by using the following scales:

   . . . .
   Like the eunuch, my coming   My coming to Christ
   was an abrupt turnaround.   was gradual.

   . . . .
   Like the eunuch, a stranger   A close friend or loved one
   gave me guidance.   "came alongside me."

   . . . .
   Like the eunuch, I was   God was searching
   searching for God.   for me.

notes:

today's session (15-20 minutes)

Share with your class the following information which you may modify according to your own perspectives and teaching needs. The answers to the student book questions (provided in the margin) are underlined.

We are warned never to pick up hitchhikers. That is generally good advice. However, in the scriptural story we are looking at today, an Ethiopian eunuch is greatly blessed by picking up a "hitchhiker," a special messenger of God who helped him with his spiritual struggle. While this is probably not a good story for us in talking about what to do with modern hitchhikers, it is an excellent story for us to discuss how to share our faith with those who are searching for the truth about God.

What aspect of this story of Philip and the eunuch is atypical of faith-sharing situations?

Admittedly, there is one aspect of this story that is somewhat atypical. As we talked about in our last session, <u>generally faith-sharing is more effective if we first develop some degree of friendship with the person with whom we are sharing</u>. This apparently did not happen in this situation. <u>Philip simply appeared to this perfect stranger and was able to show him how to begin a relationship with Jesus Christ</u>. However, Philip had a number of things going for him that helped to counteract this lack of familiarity with the eunuch. Let's look at some of these things.

Important Factors in Philip's Faith-Sharing

What were the five important factors in Philip's faith-sharing?

<u>Philip went to someone God had prepared to hear him</u>. The man had gone to Jerusalem to worship. He was what was known as a "God-fearer," a Gentile who had come to the faith of the Jews, seeking answers to questions he could not find answers for in his native religions. He was one of the ones Jesus referred to when He said, "Blessed are those who hunger and thirst for righteousness" (Matt. 5:6). How did Philip know the eunuch was ready? The text seems to indicate that it was because he was sensitive to God's guidance (vv. 26–29). Once he got close enough to the chariot, he could also tell that the man was reading Scripture, another indication that he was seeking answers.

We, too, need to be sensitive to God's guidance as to which persons He has made ready for our faith-sharing. Certainly we cannot always know for sure, and, if in doubt, we should go ahead and share. It's better to experience some rejection than let a spiritually hungry person pass us by without responding to their need. <u>However, indiscriminately trying to witness to a person who is simply not ready can harden them against the gospel, as well as getting them irritated with us. This is what Jesus was referring to when He cautioned against throwing our "pearls to pigs" (Matt. 7:6)</u>.

Why can it be a problem to witness indiscriminately to a person who is not ready? What saying of Jesus was this related to in the presentation?

<u>Philip was also obedient to the Holy Spirit's leading (v. 29)</u>. Not only did the Spirit lead him to the right person at the right time, but the Spirit also gave him the right things to say. Jesus promised us such

11

today's session (cont'd)

insight so that we don't have to think it all rests on our own eloquence or lack of it (see Matt. 10:19–20). Yet even as Christians, many of us resist the Spirit's leading in witnessing situations. <u>One way we do this is by backing down when we should speak</u>. We can feel the pull of the Spirit to say something, but our fears keep us silent. We are afraid of being rejected. We are afraid of being thought of as "religious fanatics." We are afraid of saying the wrong thing. These fears come because we are relying on our own wisdom and ability instead of relying on the Spirit's guidance and power.

What two ways of resisting the Spirit's leading are mentioned?

<u>Another way of resisting the Spirit's leading, however, is barging ahead when the Spirit is seeking to rein us in</u>. We are driven by our own needs—our need to be argumentative with someone who doesn't see "how right we are"; our need to "put another notch on our belt" by leading someone to Christ—whether they want to go or not; our need to fulfill our vision of what a believer should act like or do. We damage our witness when we witness for any of these reasons. To obey the leading of the Spirit is to respond to the spiritual need of the other person.

<u>Another factor in Philip's faith-sharing was that he knew Scripture well enough to use it</u>. Had Philip been ignorant of the passage that the Ethiopian eunuch was reading, they would have only been able to pool their ignorance. However, since he knew Scripture, Philip was able not only to answer the eunuch's questions about what he was reading, but he probably also was able to show him other relevant Scriptures. (Our text tells us that Philip "began with that very passage of Scripture.") Of course, the eunuch had already evidenced an interest in Scripture. Sometimes when all someone shows is a spiritual curiosity, it can be a mistake to bombard them with Scriptures. In such cases it might be better to use just a few short scriptural references to show that what you are saying truly is a fact from the Bible. For a person who is wary, doing more can seem like insensitive "Bible-thumping."

What else might a spiritually searching person be looking for, other than a way to heaven?

<u>Philip also showed he was wise in his manner of witnessing by responding to the questions and needs of the man to whom he was witnessing (vv. 31,34)</u>. There is a sign that says, "I know all the answers—it's the questions I don't understand!" That is the way some people witness. They try to give the answers when they don't even understand what the person's questions are yet. Not everyone who is spiritually searching is looking for a way to heaven or a way of dealing with death. <u>Some people are looking for what gives meaning to life. Some people are looking for a way of dealing with their guilt</u>—quite apart from issues of heaven and hell. And, yes,

some people are looking for answers about death and what comes after. But we have to hear the questions first. The eunuch was looking at a Scripture that dealt with suffering and its relationship to sin. Isaiah 53 tells us that Christ, though He was innocent Himself, would suffer to pay the penalty for the sins of the rest of us. That this message spoke to a need in the eunuch was evidenced by the fact that he was looking so carefully at this passage in the first place and by his later willingness to believe and be baptized.

<u>Finally, Philip's witness focused on Jesus and the good news of the Messiah's birth, life, death, and resurrection (v. 35)</u>. Witnessing that focuses on how "good" we are or what we have accomplished spiritually is always inappropriate because it smacks of self-righteousness, and it often makes the other person feel spiritually inadequate or put down. <u>Witnessing that focuses on Jesus helps people know that none of us can do it on our own</u>. We are all sinners who have been given forgiveness, and God has responded to our need through His Son, Jesus Christ.

On what should faith-sharing focus if it is to be effective?

Effective Faith-Sharing

To summarize what we have learned through this first-century story, we might say that effective faith-sharing never focuses on us. Rather, it focuses on the other person's needs and what Jesus can do for him or her spiritually. Because the kind of "ground" in which we sow our seed varies (Matt. 13:1–23), there will always be those who reject our message and those who are even angered by it. However, the more we stray from this approach, the more anger and hardness of heart our sharing will generate. The more we conform to this approach, the more we will know the joy of helping someone find answers for spiritual hunger in Jesus Christ.

notes:

11

Remain in groups of 6–8 people, in a horseshoe configuration.

In this small-group session, students will be applying the lessons of the text to their own lives through the following questions.

The students were asked (in the student book) to choose an answer for each question and explain why.

Learning from the Story (5-7 minutes)

1. The most important factor in the success of Philip's witness to this Ethiopian was:

   ☐ God had prepared the eunuch to be receptive.
   ☐ Philip was obedient to the Spirit's leading.
   ☐ Philip knew the Scripture, so he could explain it.
   ☐ Philip responded to the questions the eunuch was asking.
   ☐ Philip's words were focused on what Jesus had done.
   ☐ other: _____

2. In relationship to your own witnessing, rate yourself in the areas related to Philip's success:

   I AM SENSITIVE TO WHO GOD HAS MADE READY:

   1   2   3   4   5   6   7   8   9   10
   I generally haven't a clue.   I almost always sense this.

   I AM OBEDIENT TO THE HOLY SPIRIT'S LEADING:

   1   2   3   4   5   6   7   8   9   10
   I often drag my heels.   I go where I'm led.

   I KNOW MY SCRIPTURE AND CAN USE IT TO HELP OTHERS:

   1   2   3   4   5   6   7   8   9   10
   Not at all.   A real strength.

   I RESPOND TO THE PERSON'S QUESTIONS AND NEEDS INSTEAD OF ASSUMING I KNOW THE ANSWERS BEFORE HEARING THE QUESTIONS:

   1   2   3   4   5   6   7   8   9   10
   Not true—   Generally true—
   I follow my own agenda.   I first hear their need.

   I FOCUS ON WHAT JESUS HAS DONE FOR US:

   1   2   3   4   5   6   7   8   9   10
   Not really.   Always!

3. Finish this sentence: After evaluating myself in this way, the area I most need to work on in relationship to my witness is:

life change lessons (5-7 minutes)

Share with the class the following thoughts on how the lessons of this text might be applied today. The answers to the student book questions (provided in the margin) are underlined unless the question requires a personal answer.

Farmers have to plan ahead if they are going to have a good harvest. They have to order enough seed. They have to consider market prices for various crops and how much per acre they will have to harvest in order to make a profit. They have to make sure they have enough help and equipment for harvest time. When it comes to "harvesting" souls for God in Jesus Christ, we have to do the same. While it is certainly true that we have to wait for and do what the Holy Spirit tells us to do, there are some things, nevertheless, that we can do ahead of time to make sure we have prepared as best we can. Here are some specific suggestions that might help:

What four steps can we take to best prepare us to share our faith?

1. <u>PRAY DAILY FOR GOD TO GUIDE YOU TO RECEPTIVE PEOPLE.</u> Include this matter whenever you have a regular prayer time. As you think of it during the day, include just a one or two line prayer for this guidance as you go about your work.

2. <u>PRAY FOR THREE OR FOUR DAYS, THEN MAKE A LIST OF PEOPLE YOU BELIEVE GOD IS LEADING YOU TO SPEAK TO.</u> Pray specifically for these people. As you encounter these people, remain sensitive to the Spirit's guidance as to what to say and when to say it. Remember, it doesn't rest on your skills or abilities—success rests on your readiness to follow the guidance of God's Spirit.

For what purpose might you want to review your spiritual story you prepared in session 1?

3. <u>REVIEW YOUR SPIRITUAL STORY YOU WROTE OUT IN SESSION 1.</u> The purpose is not to have something to recite from memory. <u>The purpose here is to have something in your mind that you can share in a natural way should the Spirit present you with an opportunity</u>. You want to be able to tell the person what led you to God, and in what ways, if any, your experience has been like theirs.

4. <u>WITNESS TO AT LEAST ONE PERSON THIS WEEK.</u> You can make a list—even check it twice!—and you can review your story and pray. But sharing your faith requires action. At some point you must do it. Pray for God's leading and that you will be sensitive to it. Then, take that first step, no matter how small or tenuous. Let someone else know how much you love Christ and what He's done for you.

11

notes:

Caring Time (15-20 minutes)

⊌ CARING TIME
Remain in groups
of 6–8 people, in
a horseshoe
configuration.

Go around the group and have each person pray for the person on his or her right. Pray especially for the person's greatest need in the area of witnessing that was expressed in question 3 of "Learning from the Story." Pray also for the Holy Spirit's guidance when witnessing. Remember to include prayers for the concerns listed on the Prayer/Praise Report.

Hand out the Prayer/
Praise Report to the
entire group. Ask each
subgroup to pray for
the empty chair. Pray
specifically for God to
guide you to someone
to bring next week to
fill that chair.

notes:

After a sufficient
time of prayer in
subgroups, close in
a corporate prayer.
Say, "Next week
we will talk about:
'Experiencing
Authentic Christian
Community.'"

Remind participants
of the daily Scripture
readings and reflective
questions found on
page 128.

BIBLE STUDY NOTES

Reference Notes

Use these notes to gain further understanding
of the text as you study on your own.

ACTS 8:26
angel

an angel of the Lord. *Angel* literally means "messenger."
the road. Two roads, one of which went through a desert area, led from Jerusalem to the old city of Gaza.

ACTS 8:27
royal official

eunuch. Eunuchs were commonly employed as royal officials. Although he was attracted to Judaism, as a eunuch he would never be allowed to fully participate in the temple worship (Deut. 23:1).
Candace. A dynastic title for the Ethiopian queen.

ACTS 8:28
ox-drawn cart

chariot. While we have visions of light war chariots racing along behind fleet Arabian horses, it is probable that the eunuch was in a slow-moving, ox-drawn cart accompanied by a retinue of servants.

ACTS 8:30

Do you understand what you are reading? This reflects how the apostles themselves could not understand the Old Testament prophecies about the Messiah until they were explained by Jesus after His resurrection.

ACTS 8:32–33
the Messiah

The eunuch was reading from Isaiah 53:7–8, a key Old Testament passage about the servant of the Lord. This particular passage underlies much of

✝

ACTS 8:32–33
the Messiah (cont'd)

ACTS 8:34
a question

ACTS 8:35
an explanation

ACTS 8:36–38
a result

ACTS 8:39
rejoice

ACTS 8:40

what Luke has already recorded about the apostles' preaching concerning the identity of Jesus.

who is the prophet talking about ... ? The eunuch's question was a common one in Jewish circles. Some thought the prophet was speaking of his own sufferings as one rejected while others thought he was speaking figuratively of Israel as a nation that suffered at the hands of its oppressors (Isa. 44:1–2). Most rabbis never attributed suffering to the Messiah. Neither had the rabbis made any connection between the suffering servant of Isaiah 53, the kingly Messiah of Isaiah 11, and the glorified Son of Man in Daniel 12. Only in Jesus' teachings did these truths come together (Luke 24:26).

Philip used this passage as a jumping off point to explain the ministry of Jesus. He undoubtedly referred the eunuch to other verses in Isaiah 53 as well as other references to the Servant in Isaiah which point out the Servant's suffering for the sake of others and how this Servant would be a light for the Gentiles. All of this would have been related to Jesus' ministry, death, and resurrection.

Philip began. Literally, "opened up his mouth." The same word is used in Acts 10:34; it connotes a solemn pronouncement.

Why shouldn't I ... ? The Greek word behind this expression also occurs in the baptismal accounts of Cornelius in Acts 10:47 and 11:16-17. It may be part of a baptismal liturgy the early church used with candidates for baptism. The strict Jew would offer at least one reason why this man was ineligible to be considered part of God's people: he was a eunuch. Although due to his castration this man could never become a Jewish proselyte (see note on v. 27), he was able to become a full member of the church through Jesus Christ. This fulfills the prophecy of Isaiah 56:3–8 which anticipates a time when both foreigners and eunuchs would be welcomed into God's household. Luke may have included this particular event to illustrate just that truth.

took Philip away. Whether this was a miraculous act of God (1 Kings 18:12), or another way of describing a command of the Spirit to Philip (v. 26) is uncertain.

rejoicing. The joy of the eunuch reflects that of the believers in Jerusalem (Acts 2:46) and Samaria (Acts 8:8), another evidence of the Spirit.

Azotus. Another city on the coast of the Mediterranean Sea, about 20 miles north of Gaza.

Caesarea. The Roman seat of power in Judea, about 60 miles up the coast from Azotus. Philip evangelized throughout the Jewish communities along the Palestinian coast of the Mediterranean.

11

¹ George Barna, *What Americans Believe* (Ventura, CA: Regal Books, 1991), 220.
² George Barna, *The Index of Leading Spiritual Indicators* (Word Publishing, 1996), 7.

Session

12

Experiencing Authentic Christian Community

Prepare for the Session

	READINGS	REFLECTIVE QUESTIONS
Monday	Ephesians 4:11	What spiritual gift has God given you?
Tuesday	Ephesians 4:12	Who have you encouraged this week?
Wednesday	Ephesians 4:13	How mature in Christ are you?
Thursday	Ephesians 4:14	How easily are you swayed by any teacher?
Friday	Ephesians 4:15–16	Can others depend on you to speak the truth in love? Why or why not?
Saturday	Ephesians 4:25–28	How often do you "let the sun go down while you are still angry"?
Sunday	Ephesians 4:29–32	Which command listed in these verses do you most need to work on?

notes:

OUR GOALS FOR THIS SESSION ARE:

U **In groups of 6–8, gather people in a horseshoe configuration.**

Make sure everyone has a name tag.

Take time to share information on class parties that are coming up as well as any relevant church events.

INTRODUCE THE ICEBREAKER ACTIVITY: The students have been given instructions in their books.

After the Icebreaker say something like, "In Christ, we are all related, and conflicts that come between us are 'All in the Family.' As in any family, we must deal with our conflicts in words and actions that bind us closer together. Today, we will look at what this means for people who are part of an authentic Christian community."

Hand out the Prayer/Praise Report. A sample copy is on pages 158-159. Have people write down prayer requests and praises. Then have the prayer coordinator collect the report and make copies for use during the Caring Time.

BIBLE STUDY
- to learn what made the Christian community of the early church strong
- to discover how a Christian community can deal with conflict in a healthy way to retain and strengthen the love in the community
- to understand what role emotional honesty plays in Christian community

LIFE CHANGE
- to affirm or encourage at least one person in each group we are part of this week
- to talk to a person in our church we need to forgive for a past offense
- to reveal one thing about ourselves that most people don't know (in the next session)

Icebreaker (10-15 minutes)

All in the Family. In each of the following pairs, check which kind of person is most likely to get you "fired up":

The Bride of Frankenstein · · · · · · · · · · · · · · · · · · Ken's Barbie
nobody mess with me!   in a fairy tale world

Lon Chaney, Jr.· Ken Griffey, Jr.
caught up in a   smooth as silk,
house of horrors   and on a roll!

George Bush, Jr. · Ted Kennedy
"compassionately conservative"   unabashedly liberal

Barbara Bush · Hilary Clinton
a supporter on the sidelines   charting my own course

Franklin Graham · Jane Fonda
following in a   always heading
parent's footsteps   in new directions

notes:

12

**LEARNING FROM
THE BIBLE**

**EPHESIANS
4:11–16, 25–32**

**Have a member of
the class, selected
ahead of time, read
the passage from
Ephesians 4:11–16.
Have another class
member, selected
ahead of time, read
Ephesians 4:25–32.**

Bible Study   (30-45 minutes)

The Scripture for this week:

¹¹It was he who gave some to be apostles, some to be prophets, some to be evangelists, and some to be pastors and teachers, ¹²to prepare God's people for works of service, so that the body of Christ may be built up ¹³until we all reach unity in the faith and in the knowledge of the Son of God and become mature, attaining to the whole measure of the fullness of Christ.

¹⁴Then we will no longer be infants, tossed back and forth by the waves, and blown here and there by every wind of teaching and by the cunning and craftiness of men in their deceitful scheming. ¹⁵Instead, speaking the truth in love, we will in all things grow up into him who is the Head, that is, Christ. ¹⁶From him the whole body, joined and held together by every supporting ligament, grows and builds itself up in love, as each part does its work. ...

²⁵Therefore each of you must put off falsehood and speak truthfully to his neighbor, for we are all members of one body. ²⁶"In your anger do not sin": Do not let the sun go down while you are still angry, ²⁷and do not give the devil a foothold. ²⁸He who has been stealing must steal no longer, but must work, doing something useful with his own hands, that he may have something to share with those in need.

²⁹Do not let any unwholesome talk come out of your mouths, but only what is helpful for building others up according to their needs, that it may benefit those who listen. ³⁰And do not grieve the Holy Spirit of God, with whom you were sealed for the day of redemption. ³¹Get rid of all bitterness, rage and anger, brawling and slander, along with every form of malice. ³²Be kind and compassionate to one another, forgiving each other, just as in Christ God forgave you.

notes:

...about today's session (5 minutes)

HONESTY AND AUTHENTICITY

Summarize these introductory remarks. Be sure to include the underlined information, which gives the answers to the student book questions (provided in the margin).

What Christian writer and author is referred to as one who had to relearn what Christian community is about?

For a number of years in the '70s and '80s <u>Keith Miller</u> was one of the most popular Christian writers and speakers in America. But then his life, including his marriage, started coming apart. He had a great deal of difficulty handling this, partly because he had been such a well-known author and speaker, and people had expected so much more of him. He had to relearn what he had earlier taught—the value of honesty and authenticity in the Christian life. Becoming part of a Christian community where openness, honesty, and acceptance were valued was instrumental in his recovery. He writes of this in his book, *The Secret Life of the Soul*: "The first time I sat in this group I was frightened and uncertain. I was almost as afraid of being known and judged by that group of strangers as I was of going back to the painful prison of my previous unreal life. ... I'd been a Christian for many years and a Christian public speaker and writer for almost thirty. But I was such a fearful loner in my heart that I felt out of place and anxious with these seemingly relaxed and unafraid people."[1] As he sat in the group and heard people honestly share things that many people in the church would have greeted with judgment, and as he saw the acceptance of the group and how people experienced God's grace and forgiveness in that group, he felt tremendous relief and healing. He also learned anew what authentic Christian community was about.

According to the leader, authentic Christian community is built around removing what from our lives?

What Keith Miller had to relearn is also what many Christians today are learning: authentic Christian community is built around remov-ing <u>the falseness from our lives, learning to "speak the truth in love" with each other, and, in the process, finding the grace and accept-ance that comes through Jesus Christ.</u> That kind of community is what we will be looking at in this session.

notes:

12

Remain in groups of 6–8 people, in a horseshoe configuration.

In this small-group session, students will be responding to the following questions.

Have the students explore these questions together.

Identifying with the Story (5-7 minutes)

1. Which of the following phrases expresses the attitude toward anger in the home where you grew up?

   ☐ "We don't get mad—we get even!"
   ☐ "Don't ever let them know you're angry—grin and bear it!"
   ☐ "Anger is dangerous—run and hide!"
   ☐ "Get it off your chest—then kiss and make up!"
   ☐ "Anger? What anger?"
   ☐ "Anger is healthy, if communicated clearly and in a spirit of love."

2. In regard to how you are handling anger right now, how would you say you are doing in terms of verse 27?

   ☐ The devil must feel he is on slippery sand!
   ☐ The devil has found some footholds, but he hasn't gotten far "off the ground."
   ☐ The devil has made it at least to base camp.
   ☐ The devil is doing some high-altitude technical climbing!
   ☐ By now he is posing for pictures on the summit!

3. How would you say your ability to handle anger has affected your ability to experience authentic Christian community?

   ☐ It's limited me to the superficial—as soon as there is conflict, I leave.
   ☐ It's destroyed some groups I've been in.
   ☐ We avoid anger in the groups I've been in.
   ☐ Working through conflict has been an important key to going to a higher level of intimacy in some groups I've been in.
   ☐ I don't see a connection between handling anger and experiencing Christian community.
   ☐ other: _____

notes:

Share with your class the following information which you may modify according to your own perspectives and teaching needs. The answers to the student book questions (provided in the margin) are underlined.

What is the "richer" meaning of the word community?

In a Christian community, what should we have in common?

What is the relationship of community to diversity?

today's session (15-20 minutes)

Many people think of the word *community* in terms of its common use to designate a place where people live in homes that are in close proximity to each other and where there may be some architectural similarity between the homes. But the original meaning of the word was far richer than that. It refers to what we have *in common* and is related to the Latin word for *fellowship*. Having a true Christian community means being bound together by our *common* faith in Jesus Christ. As we look at our Scripture for this week, we can see what characteristics help build that community.

Our Common Faith

In a Christian community, what we have in *common* is our faith in Jesus Christ. We believe that Jesus is God's Son, and that as God's Son He revealed who God is. His death and resurrection bought our forgiveness from sin and freedom from the power of death. Now, as we look at the variety of denominations in Christianity, and even the variety of perspectives within each denomination, we cannot pretend that Christians have a single belief system in common. In fact, that is probably not even true within any given congregation. Community, then, does not rule out diversity, but the diversity is held together by one common belief so powerful it overrides all else—like a star that holds its various planets in orbit. In a Christian community that one belief is the belief in Jesus Christ. He is like the head of a physical body (v. 15) where, as Paul writes in our text, "From him the whole body, joined and held together by every supporting ligament, grows and builds itself up in love, as each part does its work" (v. 16).

Qualities that Strengthen the Community

In his letter to the Ephesians, Paul refers to some other qualities which help strengthen a Christian community. The first of these is *that all in the community use their gifts for the common good*. Paul lists a few of these gifts in verse 11, and then says in verse 12 that they are to be used "to prepare God's people for works of service, so that the body of Christ may be built up." The body of Christ is built up when all the organs and limbs are doing their part, functioning together. Every part is not the same. Rather, each uses its differences to contribute to the body's effective function (see 1 Cor. 12:12–26). In a Christian community, one person contributes with the gift of hospitality and another contributes with the gift of teaching, while still another enriches through the gift of encouragement. But all is done to build the body of Christ.

12

today's session (cont'd)

A second important quality Paul refers to is *striving for spiritual maturity*. He encourages people to reach for a time when they will "no longer be infants, tossed back and forth by the waves, and blown here and there by every wind of teaching and by the cunning and craftiness of men in their deceitful scheming." Spiritual immaturity can disrupt community or create a spiritual apathy that robs it of power. This is not to say that *new* Christians cannot be part of a close Christian community. The key is for people to be striving for spiritual maturity, to be seeking to grow. When people are growing, both the individual and the group are enriched.

A third community-building quality is *honesty and openness in the group*. Verse 15 talks about the need to "speak the truth in love," and verse 25 calls us to "put off falsehood and speak truthfully" to one another. People who are false with each other can *act* close, but others soon discover that it is a charade. *Acting* close means smiling when we are angry. It means saying what we think the other person expects us to say. It means not challenging their ideas out of fear of creating a rift. On the other hand, *being* close means being able to talk through our anger and finding a new appreciation for the other person in the process. It means trusting the relationship enough to really say what we think and listening to the other persons' ideas, even when they challenge our own. A famous line that Jack Nicholson's character said in *A Few Good Men*, was "Truth? You can't handle the truth!" In a Christian community, we speak the truth in love because we know that the bond of God's love is strong enough to "handle the truth."

A fourth community-building quality is related to this honesty—*conflict and anger are handled in healthy ways*. Most of us are all too familiar with unhealthy ways of handling anger: physically assaulting another, verbal abuse, passive-aggressive behavior where we quietly undermine our target, or blowing up like a volcano after trying to hold it all in, etc. Some people often equate the emotion of anger with such unhealthy expressions. But anger is just another God-given emotion. In itself it is neither good nor bad, in fact, sometimes it is appropriate. Even Jesus got angry at times (see Matt. 21:12–13). But there are ways of expressing anger that are wrong. Paul says here, "In your anger do not sin" (v. 26). This verse in the New Revised Standard Version says, "Be angry but do not sin." So it is not the anger that is wrong, but the way of expressing anger. We sin when we nurse anger so that it simmers inside us (v. 26) or when we express it by saying terrible things about the other person (v. 29), or when we let it rage out of control (v. 31). The best way to handle it

How can spiritual immaturity hurt Christian community?

If we have God's love within us, what will we be strong enough to handle?

What are some unhealthy ways of handling anger?

is to talk about it as soon as possible with the other person before it gets out of hand (v. 26). When anger is handled in such a healthy way, people understand each other more deeply, and learn to respect each other's boundaries. Both help develop community.

On the other hand, it is also true that community is developed when *people encourage each other and communication is positive*. Paul says that we should seek to talk in a way that is "helpful for building others up according to their needs, that it may benefit those who listen" (v. 29). If all we ever do is work at what has made us angry, community will not get very far. We must learn to build each other up with positive words. This is certainly in line with what we learned in sessions 7 and 8.

Finally, a quality that Christian community should always have at its heart is *forgiveness*. "Be kind and compassionate to one another, forgiving each other, just as in Christ God forgave you" (v. 32). This is the logical end of what we talked about earlier. When we get angry with each other (v. 26), we speak "the truth in love" (v. 15) so that the issue is out on the table. In that speaking, we don't say anything that tears the other person down (v. 29). That makes it easier to come to an understanding and truly forgive the other person for what he or she has done. While such forgiveness can be difficult when a hurt has cut us deeply, we look to Christ, the One who has purchased *our* forgiveness for far greater offenses, and in so doing through the Holy Spirit we can forgive others. That is what Christian community is about.

notes:

12

Remain in groups
of 6–8 people, in
a horseshoe
configuration.

**In this small-group
session, students will
be applying the lessons
of the text to their
own lives through the
following questions.**

**The students were
asked (in the student
book) to choose an
answer for each
question and
explain why.**

Learning from the Story (5-7 minutes)

1. Which of the factors mentioned in this passage do you see as most important to establishing authentic Christian community? (Rank them from "1"—most important to "7"—least important.)

   ____ All are using their gifts for the common good (vv. 11–12,16).

   ____ There is an agreement on basic beliefs (v. 13).

   ____ People in the group are striving for spiritual maturity (v. 14).

   ____ People can speak honestly to each other (vv. 15,25).

   ____ Conflict and anger are handled in healthy ways (vv. 26–27).

   ____ People encourage each other and communication is positive (v. 29).

   ____ God's forgiveness is at the heart of the group (v. 32).

2. How would you rank *this group* on these factors? (Rank them from "1"—a real strength to "5"—a real weakness.)

   ____ All are using their gifts for the common good (vv. 11–12,16).

   ____ There is an agreement on basic beliefs (v. 13).

   ____ People in the group are striving for spiritual maturity (v. 14).

   ____ People can speak honestly to each other (vv. 15,25).

   ____ Conflict and anger are handled in healthy ways (vv. 26–27).

   ____ People encourage each other and communication is positive (v. 29).

   ____ God's forgiveness is at the heart of the group (v. 32).

3. In the spirit of verse 29, what is one word of affirmation you could give to build up the person on your right?

notes:

life change lessons (5-7 minutes)

In doing the exercises of this session, we have already started applying what we have learned—being honest and open in positive ways and encouraging one another. But community should not be limited to one session. We need to build it from week to week, as intimacy grows. Of course, this is the next to last session in this study, but we want to take the learning from this session into future groups as well. Here are some suggestions:

1. AFFIRM OR ENCOURAGE AT LEAST ONE PERSON IN EACH GROUP YOU ARE PART OF THIS WEEK. This will start building positive communication as a habit that goes beyond one group. The group might be a committee, a choir you are part of, a Bible study, or whatever. Make sure that what you say is sincere. False, contrived affirmation can actually hurt community.

2. TALK TO A PERSON WHOM YOU NEED TO FORGIVE FOR A PAST OFFENSE. Let the person know what he or she did that hurt you, but assure the person also that making your relationship right is important to you. Talk about what you can both do to avoid having such problems in the future. This can be a difficult process, so be sure to pray about it before you approach the person.

3. IN THE NEXT SESSION, REVEAL ONE THING ABOUT YOURSELF THAT MOST PEOPLE DON'T KNOW. This can be in response to one of the questions, or something you share during the Caring Time. The idea is to be a little more honest and open about who you are.

notes:

Caring Time (15-20 minutes)

During this time, thank God for the positive aspects of community that you have achieved in your group. Pray that God will work in your group to create honest, authentic community. Also, use the Prayer/Praise Report and pray for the concerns listed.

Margin notes:

Share with the class the following thoughts on how the lessons of this text might be applied today. The answers to the student book questions (provided in the margin) are underlined unless the question requires a personal answer.

What groups will you be part of in the next week where you might practice encouragement and affirmation?

Who do you need to talk to in order to forgive them?

⚘ CARING TIME
Remain in groups of 6–8 people, in a horseshoe configuration.

Hand out the Prayer/Praise Report to the entire group. Ask each subgroup to pray for the empty chair. Pray specifically for God to guide you to someone to bring next week to fill that chair.

After a sufficient time of prayer in subgroups, close in a corporate prayer. Say, "Next week we will talk about: 'A Legacy in God's Kingdom.'"

Remind participants of the daily Scripture readings and reflective questions found on page 140.

12

137

BIBLE STUDY NOTES

Reference Notes

Use these notes to gain further understanding
of the text as you study on your own.

EPHESIANS 4:11

This is one of several lists of gifts in Scripture (see also Rom. 12:6–8; 1 Cor. 12:8–10,28–30). No single list is exhaustive, defining all the gifts. Each is illustrative. The emphasis in this list is on teaching gifts.

apostles

apostles. Paul probably had in mind the small group of men who had seen the resurrected Christ and had been commissioned by Him to launch His church (see Acts 1:21–22; 1 Cor. 9:1). These would include the 12 disciples (1 Cor. 15:5) and a few others (e.g. Rom. 16:7).

prophets

prophets. In contrast to teachers who relied upon the Old Testament Scripture and the teaching of Jesus to instruct others, prophets offered words of instruction, exhortation, and admonition that were immediate and unpremeditated. Their source was direct revelation from God. These prophecies were often directed to specific situations. At times, however, their words related to the future (Acts 11:27–28).

evangelists

evangelists. In the early centuries of the church, these were the men and women who moved from place to place, telling the gospel message to those who had not heard it and/or believed it. While all Christians are called upon to be witnesses of the gospel, the reference here is to those with the special gift of evangelism. This gift is the ability to make the gospel clear and convincing to many people.

pastors and teachers

pastors and teachers. The way in which this is expressed in Greek indicates that these two functions reside in one person. In a day when books were rare and expensive, it was the task of the pastor/teacher not only to look after the welfare of the flock (the title *pastor* literally means "shepherd") but to preserve the Christian tradition and instruct people in it.

EPHESIANS 4:12
ministry

prepare. These teaching gifts are to be used to train everyone in the church so that each Christian is capable of ministry. In other words, the prime task of the clergy is to train the laity to do ministry. In 3:12, Paul taught the concept of the "priesthood of all believers." Here he teaches "the ministry of all believers."

EPHESIANS 4:13–16
maturity

The aim of all these gifts is to produce maturity. Maturity is, in turn, vital to unity—the theme with which Paul began this section.

EPHESIANS 4:15
truth

speaking the truth in love. Christians are to stand for both truth and love. Both are necessary. Truth without love becomes harsh. Love without truth becomes weak.

EPHESIANS 4:25
negatives
and positives

Therefore. This verse is a model for how Paul will discuss each of six topics. He begins with the negative deed, in this case, falsehood. (In Greek the word is literally "the lie.") Then he sets in contrast the positive virtue which he commends, in this case, truthful speech. Then he gives the reason for the command. Here the reason is that we are all neighbors. In fact, we are

✝

EPHESIANS 4:25 (cont'd)

even closer than that, "we are all members of one body, the body of Christ." Lies destroy fellowship. Unity must be built on trust and trust comes via truth.

EPHESIANS 4:26
anger

In your anger. Paul recognizes that there is such a thing as legitimate anger. Paul says in 5:6 that God experiences anger, though the translation obscures the meaning. (Although the phrase in 5:6 is rendered as "God's wrath," the same word there is here translated "anger.") Jesus was angry (Mark 3:5). There are certain situations where anger is the only honest response. For Christians to deny their anger is dangerous and self-defeating. But once admitted, anger is to be dealt with, and so Paul gives four instructions on how to express anger. First, "in your anger do not sin." What is sinful is not being angry, but rather expressing it in a destructive way, by seeking to injure or destroy the person you are angry with. Second, "Do not let the sun go down on your anger," that is, deal with it quickly. Do not nurse anger and let it grow. Third, do not let anger develop into resentment. This is what the word translated "angry" at the end of verse 26 means. Get the anger out in the open. Be reconciled if possible. Apologize if it is appropriate. Fourth, "do not give the devil a foothold." Do not let Satan exploit your anger, turning it into hostility or using it to disrupt fellowship.

EPHESIANS 4:28

It is not enough simply to stop stealing; the thief must also start working.

EPHESIANS 4:29–30
good words

From the use of one's hands, Paul turns to the use of one's mouth. The word translated "unwholesome" means "rotten" and is used to describe spoiled fruit (as in Matt. 12:33). Instead of rancid words that wound others, the words of Christians ought to edify ("building others up"), be appropriate ("according to their needs"), bring grace (this is the literal rendering of the word translated "benefit"), and not distress the Holy Spirit (by unholy words).

EPHESIANS 4:31
bad attitudes

Paul identifies six negative expressions of anger which must be erased from the Christian life.
bitterness. Spiteful, long-standing resentment.
rage and anger. These two attitudes are related. The first is anger that is out of control in terms of how it is expressed, and the second is a more long-term, sullen hostility, where unexpressed anger has been allowed to grow in violation of what Paul said in verse 26.
brawling. Out-of-control, physical expression of anger.
slander. Anger expressed through verbal abuse.
malice. Wishing or plotting evil against another.

EPHESIANS 4:32
positive attitudes

In contrast to the negative attitudes listed in verse 31, here Paul identifies a set of positive attitudes that ought to characterize the Christian. Instead of negative expressions of anger, the Christian ought to be kind, compassionate, and forgiving.

12

[1] J. Keith Miller, *The Secret Life of the Soul* (Nashville, TN: Broadman and Holman Publishers, 1999), 179-80.

Session

13

A Legacy in **God's Kingdom**

Prepare for the Session

	READINGS	REFLECTIVE QUESTIONS
Monday	1 Corinthians 3:5	Do you see yourself as a servant? Why or why not?
Tuesday	1 Corinthians 3:6–8	What have you planted or watered for God?
Wednesday	1 Corinthians 3:9–11	Is your life built squarely on the foundation of Jesus Christ?
Thursday	1 Corinthians 3:12–13	What materials are you using to build your life?
Friday	1 Corinthians 3:14–15	What reward are you most looking forward to receiving from God?
Saturday	1 Corinthians 3:10–17	How can you promote unity among the Christians you know?
Sunday	John 4:27–42	What can you do this week to help bring in the "harvest"?

notes:

🐴 **In groups of 6–8, gather people in a horseshoe configuration.**

Make sure everyone has a name tag.

Take time to share information on class parties that are coming up as well as any relevant church events.

INTRODUCE THE ICEBREAKER ACTIVITY: The students have been given instructions in their books.

After the Icebreaker say something like, "In this final session we want to look back as well as look forward. We'll look back at what kind of group we have been. And we'll look forward at what kind of legacy we want to leave when our lives are complete."

Hand out the Prayer/Praise Report. A sample copy is on pages 158-159. Have people write down prayer requests and praises. Then have the prayer coordinator collect the report and make copies for use during the Caring Time.

BIBLE STUDY	• to consider what kind of legacy we can have as Christians when we do God's work
	• to learn what 1 Corinthians says about ways we can help build God's kingdom
	• to review what we have learned in previous sessions and see how using our learning is important to our legacy
LIFE CHANGE	• to make a "will" that includes the spiritual qualities we would like to leave our families when we die
	• to post a plan for "upgrading our building material" on our refrigerators or in some other visible place
	• to periodically, such as once a month, write ourselves a "building progress evaluation"

Icebreaker (10-15 minutes)

My Small Group Is ... How would you describe your small group? Choose one of the images below that you think best describes your small group. Then go around your group and explain why you chose the one you did.

LITTER OF PUPPIES: We are a fun, friendly, and enthusiastic bundle of joy; I feel younger every time we are together.

SIX MUSKETEERS: It's "all for one and one for all" with this group; I always feel that I belong and that I'm part of a great team.

M*A*S*H UNIT: This group is like a field hospital; I came in wounded, and now I feel so much better—I have a bunch of friends to boot!

ORCHARD: Whenever I'm in this group, I feel like a fragrant, healthy apple tree because of all the growing I've done, and all the fruit I've been able to share.

OASIS: While the rest of the world can be so harsh and unforgiving, this group is a refreshing stop on the journey of life.

BIRD'S NEST: I know how a baby bird feels, because being part of this group makes me feel nurtured and protected.

TEEPEE: We couldn't stand tall and provide warmth and shelter if we didn't lean on each other.

13

LEARNING FROM THE BIBLE

1 CORINTHIANS 3:5–15

Have a class member, selected ahead of time, read Paul's words to the Corinthian church in 1 Corinthians.

Bible Study (30-45 minutes)

The Scripture for this week:

⁵*What, after all, is Apollos? And what is Paul? Only servants, through whom you came to believe—as the Lord has assigned to each his task.* ⁶*I planted the seed, Apollos watered it, but God made it grow.* ⁷*So neither he who plants nor he who waters is anything, but only God, who makes things grow.* ⁸*The man who plants and the man who waters have one purpose, and each will be rewarded according to his own labor.* ⁹*For we are God's fellow workers; you are God's field, God's building.*

¹⁰*By the grace God has given me, I laid a foundation as an expert builder, and someone else is building on it. But each one should be careful how he builds.* ¹¹*For no one can lay any foundation other than the one already laid, which is Jesus Christ.* ¹²*If any man builds on this foundation using gold, silver, costly stones, wood, hay or straw,* ¹³*his work will be shown for what it is, because the Day will bring it to light. It will be revealed with fire, and the fire will test the quality of each man's work.* ¹⁴*If what he has built survives, he will receive his reward.* ¹⁵*If it is burned up, he will suffer loss; he himself will be saved, but only as one escaping through the flames.*

notes:

Summarize these introductory remarks. Be sure to include the underlined information, which gives the answers to the student book questions (provided in the margin).

What is one unsatisfying way of seeking a legacy that is referred to in the presentation?

...about today's session (5 minutes)

A GODLY LEGACY

The American landscape is dotted <u>with memorials</u>. Everywhere you go there are buildings, streets, cornerstones, and foundations, all named after dead people. Anyone expecting to raise money for any kind of structure needs to expect to put up a plaque with donor names or dedicate a walkway with names of donors carved or etched into it in a way that gives the illusion of permanence. For many people, this is what it means to have a legacy, and like "eternal" life in the era of the Egyptian Pharaohs, it is something available primarily to the wealthy. But does this really satisfy what people are looking for when they seek a legacy? Greg Bourgond,

dean of academic affairs at Bethel Seminary in St. Paul, Minnesota, writes in *Heart and Mind* magazine, "Many men and women reach the pinnacle of success as evidenced by awards and rewards only to find that their efforts didn't produce the anticipated satisfaction. Although the world applauded their accomplishments, something deep inside told them it was a mirage of little lasting substance." He later concludes, "The road to living and leaving a godly legacy is found through the disciplines of a godly life."[1]

How do we live our lives in such a way that the people we influence and the accomplishments we are part of live on when every brick is ground to dust, every building is toppled, and there is no human work left on which to put a plaque? Such a legacy can be had only by contributing to <u>the building of the kingdom of God</u>. In this final session we will look at what this means.

A truly lasting legacy can be had only through contributing to what?

notes:

U **Remain in groups of 6–8 people, in a horseshoe configuration.**

In this small-group session, students will be responding to the following questions.

Have the students explore these questions together.

Identifying with the Story (5-7 minutes)

1. Finish this sentence with one of the endings that follow it: "During my lifetime, I have spent the most time and effort building ... ."

   ☐ debt!   ☐ relationships
   ☐ my power base   ☐ memories
   ☐ actual buildings   ☐ my reputation
   ☐ faith   ☐ family
   ☐ frustration   ☐ other:_____

2. What "Apollos" has been building alongside you, sometimes building on what you have done, and sometimes vice versa?

3. What have you achieved to this point in your life that you believe will have the greatest staying power—something that will last beyond a few years?

13

today's session (15-20 minutes)

When it comes to building the church, no one in history (apart from Jesus Christ) has had more influence than the apostle Paul. Over half of the book of Acts details his missionary work, and his letters to churches make up most of the New Testament. He was probably the first to take the good news about Jesus' life, death, and resurrection into Europe where it thrived and was transmitted to cultures all over the world. From being a man whose name would probably have disappeared from history as a persecutor of the church, the name of Paul of Tarsus is now one of the most recognized by Christian cultures all over the world. So his thoughts on building something permanent certainly should have some weight with us.

Paul shared his thoughts on building something that will last in this letter to the Corinthians. He shared these thoughts in the context of a conflict. The Christians of Corinth had divided into factions. Some said they had loyalty to Paul. Some said they had loyalty to Peter. Some followed the leadership of Apollos, and some apparently went their own way, saying they followed only Christ (see 1 Cor. 1:10–17). In the midst of this conflict, <u>Paul told them that they all needed to be on the same building crew, working together in Jesus' name, to build something that would have eternal significance</u>. Let's look at some of the insights he shared in relationship to this.

What message was Paul trying to get across to the factions in Corinth?

God at the Center

The first thing Paul says is the ironic truth that if you want to have your achievements last, they *can't be centered on you*—they have to be centered on God. "What, after all, is Apollos? And what is Paul? Only servants" (v. 5). Had what Paul and Apollos been doing been centered on themselves and building a reputation for themselves, it would have never lasted. But they were servants, each contributing his part to the kingdom of God. Just a short time earlier, <u>King Herod the Great</u> lived and was known as a great builder in Jerusalem. <u>But everything he built was leveled in A.D. 70. His building had focused on glorifying his own name</u>. The only thing that survives in the minds of most people regarding King Herod is that he was the one responsible for the "slaughter of the innocents" in Bethlehem after Jesus' birth (Matt. 2:16). Paul and Apollos weren't kings, but the church they helped build is for eternity. <u>It is for eternity because it is not founded on self, but on Jesus Christ</u>: "For no one can lay any foundation other than the one already laid, which is Jesus Christ" (v. 11).

What example is given of a builder who lived a little before Paul and Apollos, whose building didn't last? Why didn't it last?

Who should our building be centered on if we want it to last?

Strategies for Building for Eternity

There are some other things we learn about building for eternity from the example of Paul and Apollos in 1 Corinthians. The first is

144

that we should *work more at building people and less at building things*. The modern church has put a lot of effort into building church buildings and putting memorial plaques all over them. But no matter how nice they are, one day they will crumble. And even though some of the great sanctuaries of Europe still stand, most of them are no longer used as churches. One day they will fall completely. The churches of Paul and Apollos, however, built no buildings. They worshiped in homes and witnessed in the marketplace. What was built was a people of God. Each person was a stone in that building (v. 9). Paul earlier referred by name to some of the "stones" he had put in place (1:14–17).

Where did the churches that Paul and Apollos built worship?

When we witness to others, when we raise our children as believers in Jesus Christ, we are building the people of God, and developing an eternal legacy. When all is said and done at the end of time, no buildings will survive. But people's souls are forever. Loving fellowship with God in Jesus Christ is what we must seek to build.

A second building strategy is related to the first: We must *build toward spiritual goals instead of just physical goals*. Even if we focus on people, we are doing temporary building if we just focus on their physical needs. Certainly physical need is important, and Jesus spent time ministering to people's physical needs. But we all die, and when we die, physical need is over. What happens then to the spirit? In addition, even a person who is still alive can be spiritually dead. That's why Jesus referred to Himself as "the bread of life" (John 6:35), and promised to feed more than people's bodies (see also John 4:32–33).

Building for eternity also means *letting Christ be our architect*. God's building is unique because Jesus Christ is both the foundation and the architect! He is the One who knows and directs us toward the final design. If builders work without consulting the design of the building, what they do most often has to be torn out and materials are wasted. The same is true when we seek to build something eternal for God in our own way.

If builders build without consulting the architect's design, what happens?

Finally, building for eternity requires that *our building be inspected*. When any new building is built in our culture, someone has to inspect it to make sure it's been built according to code. Scripture tells us that something similar happens when we build for God. Verses 13–15 of our text tells us that when a person builds, "his work will be shown for what it is, because the Day will bring it to light. It will be revealed with fire, and the fire will test the quality of each man's work. If what he has built survives, he will receive his reward. If it is burned up, he will suffer loss."

13

today's session (cont'd)

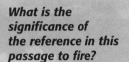

What is the significance of the reference in this passage to fire?

The image of fire was a common one for trial or judgment in ancient times. <u>What can survive fire is what is truly valuable and permanent.</u> <u>Paul was saying that God's way of inspecting our building is by checking it for permanence.</u> If a builder knows his or her building is going to be inspected and that they will have to redo what is not according to code, doesn't he or she inspect it first? That is why we should periodically take time to "inspect" our lives for how we are building. Are we building with inferior materials that won't survive the fire? Is what we are working for just the day-to-day goal of survival, or are we building something eternal and spiritual, according to what God has revealed to us? This question can better be answered if we look back at how we are doing at the other concerns we have looked at in this course. Are we living authentically, disciplining ourselves like an athlete? Are we loving and ministering to the needs of the people around us? Are we reaching out to the unchurched, sharing our faith in Jesus Christ so that they, too, might believe in Him and find eternal hope? If we are, then we are truly building with gold, silver, and precious stones.

notes:

Remain in groups of 6–8 people, in a horseshoe configuration.

In this small-group session, students will be applying the lessons of the text to their own lives through the following questions.

The students were asked (in the student book) to choose an answer for each question and explain why.

Learning from the Story (5-7 minutes)

1. As you evaluate what you have done to this point in your life, which of the materials that Paul mentions in this passage would you say you are "building with"?

   ☐ Gold—Much of what I'm doing will have a lasting, valuable impact for God.

   ☐ Silver—I can point to several things I have accomplished which will have a lasting, positive impact for God.

   ☐ Costly Stones—I haven't been a "world-changer," but I have had a positive, desirable impact on my little corner.

   ☐ Wood—I've worked mostly for common goals, just making it from day to day, but with a few more lasting accomplishments.

   ☐ Hay or Straw—I've never done anything that has meant much.

2. In order to "upgrade your building material," which of the following do you most need to do?

   ☐ work more at building people instead of building things
   ☐ work more at spiritual goals instead of just physical goals
   ☐ let Christ be my architect, directing how I build
   ☐ take time to evaluate my life, to be more intentional in the goals I am working toward
   ☐ other: _____

3. To strengthen your legacy, what do you most need to work on?

   ☐ being authentic and not hypocritical (session 3)
   ☐ using spiritual disciplines (session 5)
   ☐ caring for others (session 6)
   ☐ encouraging and affirming others (sessions 7 and 8)
   ☐ ministering to those in need (session 9)
   ☐ building relationships with unchurched friends (session 10)
   ☐ sharing my faith (session 11)

notes:

13

life change lessons (5-7 minutes)

People plan carefully when it comes to what they will leave their family in their will. They talk to family members to determine what each person would like to have left to them. <u>They consult lawyers to make sure what they want is said in words that will leave no room for loopholes. If they have favorite charities or church-related ministries, they make sure they are also included. And they may even seek advice on how to do these things while minimizing the tax their survivors have to pay on inheritance. If we plan that carefully on the physical things we leave, we should also plan that diligently in regard to our spiritual legacy.</u> Here are some things we can do to accomplish that:

1. MAKE A "WILL" THAT INCLUDES THE SPIRITUAL QUALITIES YOU WOULD LIKE TO LEAVE YOUR FAMILY WHEN YOU DIE. This is for your own benefit, so that you can focus on the things you must do now to make sure this "will" is carried out. However, you may also want to show it to your family members.

2. POST A PLAN FOR "UPGRADING YOUR BUILDING MATERIAL" ON YOUR REFRIGERATOR OR IN SOME OTHER VISIBLE PLACE. You may want to consult your responses to questions 2 and 3 under "Learning from the Story" to write out this plan. This will help keep you focused on what you truly want to build with your life.

3. <u>PERIODICALLY, SUCH AS ONCE A MONTH, WRITE YOURSELF A "BUILDING PROGRESS EVALUATION."</u> This could be written in a personal journal. Affirm yourself for what you have done that you believe has permanent value for God. Give yourself an evaluation in the terms of Paul's instruction to the Corinthians. Have you built this month with gold, silver, precious stones, wood, hay, or straw?

Share with the class the following thoughts on how the lessons of this text might be applied today. The answers to the student book questions (provided in the margin) are underlined unless the question requires a personal answer.

What are some things people consider when making out their wills? What are the implications of this planning for your spiritual legacy?

How often does the leader advise that you do a "building progress evaluation"?

notes:

148

PRAYER OF COMMITMENT

"Lord Jesus, I need you. I realize I'm a sinner, and I can't save myself. I need Your mercy. I believe that You are the Son of God, that You died on the cross for my sins and rose from the dead. I repent of my sins and put my faith in You as Savior and Lord. Take control of my life, and help me follow You in obedience. In Jesus' name. Amen."

Caring Time   (15-20 minutes)

CARING TIME
Remain in groups of 6–8 people, in a horseshoe configuration.

Hand out the Prayer/Praise Report to the entire group. Be sure to allow enough time for the evaluation. If your group is going to continue, also allow time to discuss the covenant on page 151. Close with a corporate prayer.

Pray for the concerns listed on the Prayer/Praise Report, then continue with the evaluation and covenant.

1. Take some time to evaluate the life of your group by using the statements below. Read the first sentence out loud and ask everyone to explain where they would put a dot between the two extremes. When you are finished, go back and give your group an overall grade in the categories of Group Building, Bible Study, and Mission.

GROUP BUILDING

On celebrating life and having fun together, we were more like a ...
wet blanket · hot tub

On becoming a caring community, we were more like a ...
prickly porcupine · cuddly teddy bear

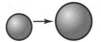

BIBLE STUDY

On sharing our spiritual stories, we were more like a ...
shallow pond · spring-fed lake

On digging into Scripture, we were more like a ...
slow-moving snail · · · · · · · · · · · · · · · · · · · voracious anteater

MISSION

On inviting new people into our group, we were more like a ...
barbed-wire fence · wide-open door

On stretching our vision for mission, we were more like an ...
ostrich · eagle

13

Caring Time (cont'd)

2. What are some specific areas in which you have grown in this course?

☐ affirming and encouraging others
☐ using my life experiences to help others
☐ being mentored and/or mentoring an emerging leader
☐ developing a daily quiet time with God
☐ finding a way to use my gifts and talents in a ministry
☐ developing a habit of studying the truths of the Bible to help me with life change
☐ other: _____

A covenant is a promise made to another in the presence of God. Its purpose is to indicate your intention to make yourselves available to one another for the fulfillment of the purposes you share in common. If your group is going to continue, in a spirit of prayer work your way through the following sentences, trying to reach an agreement on each statement pertaining to your ongoing life together. Write out your covenant like a contract, stating your purpose, goals, and the ground rules for your group.

1. The purpose of our group will be:

2. Our goals will be:

3. We will meet on _____ (day of week).

4. We will meet for _____weeks, after which we will decide if we wish to continue as a group.

5. We will meet from _____ to _____ and we will strive to start on time and end on time.

6. We will meet at _____ (place) or we will rotate from house to house.

✝

7. We will agree to the following ground rules for our group (check):

☐ PRIORITY: While you are in this course of study, you give the group meetings priority.

☐ PARTICIPATION: Everyone is encouraged to participate and no one dominates.

☐ RESPECT: Everyone has the right to his or her own opinion, and all questions are encouraged and respected.

☐ CONFIDENTIALITY: Anything said in the meeting is never repeated outside the meeting.

☐ LIFE CHANGE: We will regularly assess our own life change goals and encourage one another in our pursuit of Christlikeness.

☐ EMPTY CHAIR: The group stays open to reaching new people at every meeting.

☐ CARE AND SUPPORT: Permission is given to call upon each other at any time, especially in times of crisis. The group will provide care for every member.

☐ ACCOUNTABILITY: We agree to let the members of the group hold us accountable to the commitments which each of us make in whatever loving ways we decide upon.

☐ MISSION: We will do everything in our power to start a new group.

☐ MINISTRY: The group will encourage one another to volunteer and serve in a ministry, and to support missions by giving financially and/or personally serving.

notes:

13

Reference Notes

Use these notes to gain further understanding
of the text as you study on your own.

BIBLE STUDY NOTES

1 CORINTHIANS 3:5
servants

servants. Paul and Apollos are not to be exalted. They are merely servants, and not of a very high order. They were simply carrying out the task God had called them to.

1 CORINTHIANS 3:6
growth

I planted. Paul was the first evangelist to preach in Corinth.
Apollos watered. Apollos continued Paul's work by assisting in the building up of the new church.
God made it grow. Their labors alone would not have been enough. The divine life-force necessary to produce growth came from God (v. 7).

1 CORINTHIANS 3:8
purpose

one purpose. Paul and Apollos were colleagues, not rivals. They had the same ultimate purpose even though they had different specific tasks to fulfill. (One began the work; the other nurtured it.)

1 CORINTHIANS 3:9

God's field. The Corinthians are the field which God is plowing via His servants.
God's building. Paul shifts the metaphor from agriculture to architecture.

1 CORINTHIANS 3:10
foundation

I laid a foundation. By preaching Christ, who is the foundation (v. 11), Paul was the one who began the work in Corinth (v. 6).
expert. Literally, "wise." This reference is reminiscent of Christ's teaching about the wisdom of building on a rock rather than on a sand foundation (Matt. 7:24–25).
builder. This is one who plans and supervises the construction of a building, not the one who does the actual labor.

1 CORINTHIANS 3:11
Jesus

A community might be built on another foundation (e.g., the leadership and ideas of a famous philosopher), but it would not be the church. The church's only foundation is the person of Jesus Christ (see 1 Cor. 1:18–25).

1 CORINTHIANS 3:12
building materials

Paul describes how a person can go astray (as he warns in v. 10) by using inferior or inadequate materials to build on the foundation.
gold, silver, costly stones. These materials will survive the test of fire.
wood, hay or straw. These will burn up.

1 CORINTHIANS 3:13
quality test

The Day. On the Day of Judgment, the quality of such labor will be revealed.
fire. The idea is not of fire as punishment but as a means of testing, a way of revealing the quality of each person's work. This is a strong warning to those who lead the church.

1 CORINTHIANS 3:15

he himself will be saved. Here it becomes evident that Paul is not writing about what threatens salvation, but rather what threatens one's legacy, one's contribution to the kingdom.

[1] Greg Bourgond, "The Significance Factor " *Heart & Mind*, Vol. 14, No. 1, 12,15

notes

notes

notes

notes

notes

Name   **Phone No.**

_____   _____

_____   _____

_____   _____

_____   _____

_____   _____

_____   _____

_____   _____

_____   _____

_____   _____

_____   _____

_____   _____

_____   _____

_____   _____

_____   _____

_____   _____

_____   _____

Pray and Praise Pages

Pray for ...   **Praise God for ...**

_____   _____

_____   _____

_____   _____

_____   _____

_____   _____

_____   _____

_____   _____

_____   _____

_____   _____

_____   _____

_____   _____

_____   _____

_____   _____

_____   _____

_____   _____

_____   _____

_____   _____